8th e-Learning Excellence Awards 2022

An Anthology of Case Histories

Edited by Dan Remenyi

8th e-Learning Excellence Awards: An Anthology of Case Histories

Copyright © 2022 The authors

First published October 2022

All rights reserved. Except for the quotation of short passages for the purposes of critical review, no part of this publication may be reproduced in any material form (including photocopying or storing in any medium by electronic means and whether or not transiently or incidentally to some other use of this publication) without the written permission of the copyright holder except in accordance with the provisions of the Copyright Designs and Patents Act 1988, or under the terms of a licence issued by the Copyright Licensing Agency Ltd, Saffron House, 6-10 Kirby Street, London EC1N 8TS. Applications for the copyright holder's written permission to reproduce any part of this publication should be addressed to the publishers.

Disclaimer: While every effort has been made by the editor, authors and the publishers to ensure that all the material in this book is accurate and correct at the time of going to press, any error made by readers as a result of any of the material, formulae or other information in this book is the sole responsibility of the reader. Readers should be aware that the URLs quoted in the book may change or be damaged by malware between the time of publishing and accessing by readers.

Note to readers: Some papers have been written by authors who use the American form of spelling and some use the British. These two different approaches have been left unchanged.

ISBN: 978-1-914587-53-5 (print)
ISBM: 978-1-914587-54-2 (pdf)

Published by: Academic Conferences International Limited, Reading, United Kingdom, info@academic-conferences.org

Available from www.academic-bookshop.com

Table of Contents

Introduction iii

Teaching Management Online with a "cine-case" 1
   Emilia Bunea

Orchestrating Technology to Create Integrated Learning Experiences
for Nursing Students 15
   Tim Cappelli

A Novel Converged Learning Model as an Agile Method for Teaching
and Learning Before, During, and After the Pandemic 35
   Fadi P. Deek and Regina Collins

Capsule: Supporting UK Undergraduate Medical Education 49
   Nadia Mahmood et al

open.uom.lk: A free online knowledge sharing platform 65
   Vishaka Nanayakkara et al

Teachers in Action: Producing, Differentiating and Digitalizing Content Lesson
Materials for Inclusive Lessons in Grades 4 and 5 81
   Lisa Paleczek et al

Using e-Learning to Support Entrepreneurs at a Time of Crisis: A South African
perspective 99
   Sweta Patnaik and Shamil Isaacs

The Data-Free Moya Messenger Application: Online Accounting Tutoring in a
Large Class 113
   Fazlyn Petersen and Ronald Arendse

Xbox: The Training Ground: Empowering Support Advocates
via Engaging Training 125
   C. Sigmund, K. Kulkarni, S. Nayar

Stop Predatory Practices – Teaching module 139
   Tereza Šímová, Zychová Kristýna Paulová Kristýna

DEUinK: Open orchestration for capacity development nationwide 151
   Denise Whitelock et al

Wright School of Business Collaborative Online International Initiative: Doing
Business in Peru* 163
   Stephen Ray Smith and Amy Burger

Acknowledgements

We would like to thank the judges, who initially read the abstracts of the case histories submitted to the competition and discussed these to select those to be submitted as full case histories. They subsequently performed double-blind evaluations of the entries and made further selections to produce the finalists who are published in this book.

Paula Charbonneau Gowdy is Associate Professor in English as a Foreign Language Teacher Education at the Universidad Andres Bello in Santiago, Chile and formerly Senior Advisor in Learning and Technology to the Government of Canada. Her research interests lie in the sociocultural implications of online learning for teaching, learning and learners.

Reet Cronk is a professor, Associate Dean of Harding Online and Director of Information Systems Graduate Studies. She holds a PhD in Information Systems and a Master of Science in Molecular Genetics. Research interests include the use of technology in education, gamification, e-learning, knowledge management, and the business value of information systems.

Colin Loughlin is the Learning Technology Manager at the University of Surrey (UK) and a PhD candidate with Lund University (Sweden). His research interests are related to large class teaching and the impact of educational theory on classroom practice. Recently published: 'Reclaiming Constructive Alignment' (bit.ly/reclaimingCA)

Susan Crichton is an emeritus professor in Educational Technologies at the University of British Columbia, Canada. She is currently a consultant who has been working to support educators in the K-12 sector, as well as post-secondary trades training and university to respond to the challenges posed by COVID 19.

Introduction

e-Learning and indeed blended learning are now established integral ways in which education and training are managed and delivered across all levels of education and in the workplace. The International e-Learning Excellence Awards provides an opportunity for individuals and groups to consider new and innovative ways of using this method of learning.

The response this year to the eighth International e-Learning Excellence Awards reflects the continuing innovation being practised in many parts of the world. With 26 initial submissions from 12 countries, 20 competitors were invited to send in a full case history describing their initiative. The range of subjects written about in the case histories has certainly been extensive and the panel of expert judges had their job cut out for them to find the most interesting case histories and short list them to the finalists published in this anthology.

11 authors or groups of authors have been invited to present their work in the final rounds of this competition at the 2022 European Conference on e-Learning, being held at the University of Brighton in the UK, and as finalists these initiatives are published in this book of case histories. The topics to be addressed are listed in the Contents page of this book and represent projects from Austria, the Czech Republic, Sri Lanka, South Africa, the United Kingdom and the United States.

I would like to thank all the contributors to the book for the excellent work which has been done towards developing new and interesting ways of applying e-Learning. And of course, it is also important to thank the individuals who constituted our panel of expert judges.

Dr Dan Remenyi
October 2022

Teaching Management Online with a "cine-case"

Emilia Bunea
CEO Ed.movie Inc., USA
emilia@ed.movie

Introduction

The case method represents the dominant management teaching approach at leading business schools (such as Harvard) and is practiced worldwide. Often starting from a real-life situation, the case usually describes a management-related challenge faced by its main protagonist and asks of students to put themselves into the shoes of the protagonist and consider and discuss how they would address this challenge. The case method promotes managerial skills such as problem solving, interpersonal skills, self-awareness (Farashahi & Tajeddin, 2018) and (a competence increasingly required of today's managers) tolerance for ambiguity (Rosier, 2022).

However, traditional case teaching is increasingly challenged. When starting from a case on paper (by necessity a linear sequence of information items), students tend to follow a purely rational path towards "solving the case", rather than experience, through the eyes of the protagonist, the complexity, ambiguity and immediacy of a real-life situation. This grossly oversimplifies the real-life experience, especially in fields such as leadership and organizational behavior. In addition, management educators complain that after a period of intense learning with cases in most of their subjects, students start mixing up the various cases, their protagonists and the corresponding learning, with deleterious consequences for retention and application of the concepts studied. Moreover, many educators (and especially those newer to case teaching) find it an increasingly daunting task to start and fuel a lively discussion between students, which is a sine qua non of successful case teaching.

The case method in an online setting

While the case method dominates in business education, it is not naturally suited to an online environment, due to its highly interactive nature. Business educators, like the rest of the world, have had to adapt to the post-Covid 19 reality and they do teach with cases online, but results are mixed. At best, successfully teaching with cases in an online environment requires even stronger skills and effort from the educator (Garcia & Cabanas, 2022). The challenges of case teaching mentioned earlier are amplified in a virtual environment. Therefore business educators are in high need for cases that are:

- More engaging than traditional paper-, or documentary style video-based cases;
- Offering emotion-based, and not only rational-based learning;
- Immersing students in realistic business situations and settings;
- Offering more flexibility for being used in an online setting.

Some leadership educators choose to address these challenges by using popular movies as discussion cases, from "Game of Thrones" (Yu & Campbell, 2021) to "The Office" (DelCampo et al., 2010). However, what popular movies can offer to leadership teaching is a repository of metaphors, not a lifelike leadership case depiction. These metaphors, albeit engaging and aiding in illustration and memorization of theoretical concepts, can only go so far. Even a film ostensibly about work, like the Office, only reminds us of the worst bosses or colleagues we might have had, in a heavily caricaturized (and irresistibly funny) way, rather than show realistic leadership development journeys or predicaments. As a result, discussing a popular movie for leadership purposes often only affords questions of the type "from the theoretical model I have taught you, what applies to this particular scene?" (see Rosser, 2007: 246 for several examples of such questions). This is certainly an engaging way to enliven traditional lecturing, but does not truly represent and bring out the benefits of case teaching.

Nevertheless, the emotional involvement, the total immersion that cinema brings, are incomparable to reading a case or even watching video interviews about it. Only cinema can truly put participants "in the shoes of the protagonist", an ideal that all case instructors aspire to, but rarely attain.

These were the considerations that led us to producing a bespoke, real life-based, cinematic quality leadership case (or "cine-case"). To our knowledge, this is the first management "cine-case", a case that combines deep business content with cinema-quality film.

"Crossroads Life" (https://www.imdb.com/title/tt15548102/?ref_=fn_al_tt_1), the movie at the center of the "cine-case", was shot in spring 2021 and finalized in post-production in September 2021. I have since taught the case to a variety of student levels, offline and online, in several countries. In what follows I will focus on the experience of producing the case and then teaching with it online.

The infrastructure

The product. The cine-case "Clara Banu at Crossroads Life" consists of:

- A 56-minute movie ("Crossroads Life"), directed and photographed by an awarded director, with a cast of 11 professional actors. The movie received numerous awards from film festivals, which demonstrates its value as a stand-alone film for non-business audiences. Although I do not intend to distribute the movie other than in an educational/leadership development context, this is an important validation of the ability of the movie to engage and immerse students, which in turn represents a key ingredient of the "cine-case" concept. To my knowledge, this makes "Clara Banu at Crossroads Life" the first of its kind;
- A five-part written case that is consistent with the movie, while they each contribute something different to the learning experience. The written case contains more business information (such as, for example, excerpts from a 360-degree feedback report of the protagonist). The movie contributes the myriad of micro-expressions on the faces of its characters, it recreates a specific atmosphere around the protagonist and the events, it shows implicit and explicit dialogue in each scene. Without the movie, the written case would suffer from the shortcomings discussed in "Introduction" above. Without the detailed business background of the written case, students could misinterpret some behaviors or expressions as seen on the screen.
- A number of simulation scenarios (11 at present but continuing to grow) whereby students are instructed to "become" one of the characters in the movie, acting in a new situation, not seen in the film/written case but consistent with the background set up by the film/written case. For example, acting as Esther, the HR director, and after being provided more background on Esther's thinking and motivations regarding the situation at hand, a student is asked to convince Henk, the CEO – played by another student or by the instructor – that he should provide additional support and training to Clara, the new CFO. Having seen the film/read the case, students realize that this will be a difficult sell given Henk's transactional leadership style and may even be able to think of what to offer Henk "in

exchange". The roleplay scenarios are designed to develop various leadership competences/worldviews (in the "Esther" example, negotiation skills and making difficult choices under pressure). These simulations take place in a – by now – familiar, complex and realistic environment for the students, the "world" of the "Crossroads Life" corporation, with its culture, business priorities, personalities and relationships. As such, these simulations are, I believe, best among simulations currently available in leadership/organizational behavior teaching and come closest to how students would behave in a real-life business situation.

- Instructor support consisting of teaching notes for the case and the simulations and a line-by-line annotated movie script. The case teaching note is attached.
- Other materials that support the teaching experience (e.g. a chart with photos of the characters in the case; comics-style sheets portraying "alternative world" scenarios involving the same characters as seen in the film, that can be used to add depth to, and enliven the case discussion; online quizzes), that we continue to add to.

Making the cine-case. Making "Clara at Crossroads Life" started where all cases start: with a case writer getting access to the details of a real-life story (usually by accessing the main protagonist) and writing down the management case. In this particular situation, the case is based on my own experience. Before getting my PhD and starting a different life, I had been an executive for over twenty years. I chose the most identity-wrenching, painful leadership transformation I had experienced. Then I interviewed six of my colleagues at the time to cross-check my recollection of the events and the context. Yet I do not claim that the story I finally put on paper reflects the "objective truth": organizations are collections of stories, and "reality" is co-constructed at any given time by those who tell the story. The resulting case presents the situation exclusively as seen through the eyes of the protagonist. Since it deals with leadership development and aims to put viewers in the protagonist's shoes, this proved to be a strength, rather than a weakness.

Future "cine-cases" (whether produced by myself of by others) will likely involve two cine-case persons (the case protagonist and the management academic) instead of one person combining the two roles, as was the case here. The management academic will need to decide how close to stay to the story as told by the case protagonist. I would recommend that, unless the story is grossly self-serving or otherwise visibly unrealistic (in which case it probably wouldn't have been selected for a case study to begin with), one should stay as close to the protagonist's representation of it as possible. Yes, it is bound to come with blank spots, implicit assumptions and personal worldviews, but also with a unique internal consistency that, once violated, is very difficult to reconstruct.

Teaching online with a cine-case

Participants can watch (parts of) the cine-case either before class or in-class, either through a screen sharing option or by receiving a link to the cine-case posted online. I chose to have participants watch the movie in class, both in order to control the viewing experience (our younger students are prone to watching any video material on a small screen and/or at 1.5 times the normal speed, which would dilute the cinema-like experience and emotional involvement of the viewer) and in order to capture that moment when students are still immersed in what they have just watched and impatient to discuss and make sense of it.

Instructors can add a "twist" to the case discussion, using the advantage of having both a written case and a movie at hand, both depicting essentially the same sequence of events. This approach is particularly effective when teaching large groups online (my largest group counted over 140 MBA students). I split the students into two groups, "viewers" and "readers". While the "viewers" watched a first segment of the film, the "readers" read the corresponding parts of the written case. After watching/reading the first part of the case, students met in breakout rooms (6-8 students per room, always a mix of "viewers" and "readers") to take part in a contest as teams, whereby they had limited time available to answer a quiz probing their understanding of what was "really going on". The ensuing exercise of debating and reaching agreement was intended to develop students' appreciation for the various ways of "knowing" (from fact-based to emotion/empathy-based) and their ability to communicate effectively, in addition to their internalizing the learning specific to the case (leadership-related topics such as leadership styles, power and politics in organizations, self-leadership, burnout and flourishing in the leader role).

The online medium requires constant variation in the tempo and the format of the learning experience. A "cine-case" is ideal for this, as it is entirely flexible: instructors can choose to stop the film anywhere and with any frequency, from very high (say, after every scene) to only 3-4 times for the whole movie (at the natural turning points of the story) and continue with discussion/debate/teamwork-based quizzes or simulations. Depending on learning outcomes and the available time, teachers can go from a "micro" approach (e.g. discussing, after a scene, "what really happened here?", "what were the emotions in the room?" "what are the motivations of the participants in the scene?") aiming to develop students' empathy and mindfulness, to a "macro" approach (e.g. discussing, after watching the full film, whether the central character has really become a better leader or only better adapted to her current, highly political environment) aiming to develop students' leadership worldviews and acceptance of paradox.

Asynchronous teaching. The first asynchronous teaching experience with the cinematic case will take place within a few days from the time we are writing this case history. We expect the cinematic case to greatly improve the asynchronous learning engagement of students and the effectiveness of the learning experience.

The challenges

Producing a cine-case presents all the challenges one encounters when producing a movie and adds the specific ones of reconciling educational aims with cinematic ones. For example, working with a professional script writer can be painfully difficult. The challenge is to reconcile the need to turn a jumble of events into a gripping story with the need to stay true to the real-life events. For example, I agreed to merging two "real" individuals into only one character in the movie, because the resulting fictional character felt almost real to me, as he embodied values and behaviors I'd often seen around at that time. But I could not agree to completely cutting the "business talk" that exasperated the script writer, because that is how people really talk in offices! While in Hollywood movies the business content, the actual work people do, is always glossed over, with centre stage given to the rivalries, friendships, romantic relationships between the characters, in a cine-case the work takes centre stage. In research we have long accepted that work is the leading source of meaning for most individuals, but in the film world this is never shown (unless the work is of "inventing an all-cancer cure"-like importance). Thus, another topic of contention may be what is really "at stake" in the film. If your film is, say, about the leadership journey of a middle manager in a corporation, what is at stake (maybe the protagonist's self-confidence or the success of a project they lead) will seem minor by Hollywood standards. But it is making the viewer feel the actual weight and meaning of such apparently minor stakes, that will prove the art and creativity of the filmmaker (and, in the process, give generations of struggling new managers something to remember, take comfort in, and draw lessons from, when they might think they are the only ones struggling with the complexity of leadership).

The challenges we faced during casting and shooting were not insignificant but would not have been any different had it not been a management movie. What is different and crucially important for a management cine-case is to have the management educator (and, if possible, the case protagonist) on the set, watching every take. This needs to be carefully managed, with clear, pre-set rules as to when the case protagonist and/or the management educator may intervene (e.g. "this would never play like that in a multinational company" is reason enough for veto;

"this is not how I imagined this scene" is not). Not having these people on set means leaving it to the director (who, more often than not, has never set foot in a corporation) to decide on what a "realistic" work scene may look like. This same arrangement should apply to post-production. In other words, if you are a management educator leading the production of a cine-case, expect to invest thousands of hours into closely monitoring it, lest the result be closer to Hollywood's idea of what goes on in organizations, than to the real-life case you have been working so hard to bring to leadership students.

How the initiative was received by participants

Students at all levels find the cine-case learning experience particularly rewarding. Masters-level students found it a "transformative experience that has connected us". Executives recognized the situations depicted in the case and the struggle of the protagonist resonated with them (as one of them put it, "I wish I had seen this film ten years ago"). Participants generally underline how valuable they found it to actually "see" the characters and the story, rather than only read about them. Those participants who had read the written case before watching the movie, were surprised at how much depth the movie added to their understanding and sense making around the case. Formal course evaluations are available upon request.

Learning outcomes

The cine-case affords a wide array of leadership-related learning outcomes, depending on the needs of the audience and the aims of the educator. The teaching note (available upon request) describes these learning outcomes, broadly covering all topics found in a leadership textbook.

However, there is an overarching learning outcome of a cine-case: having students put themselves in the shoes of the protagonist (so that they internalize all other learning outcomes more deeply), more than they would when teaching with a pdf case only. To test this outcome, we set up an experiment as described below.

Empirical study

Setting. In order to assess the impact of the cine-case as compared to a traditional written case, we conducted a randomized experiment. We did so in the context of teaching a 6-hour synchronous online leadership development module for Post Graduate Diploma in Management students at a large business school in India. Specifically, we randomly assigned 72 management students to either viewing the Crossroads Life film ("viewers") or to reading the corresponding pdf case ("readers").

Hypotheses. We hypothesised 1) that viewing the film would be more effective in "putting students into the shoes of the protagonist" than reading the pdf case. To that end, we asked students whether they believed they would have navigated the situation depicted in the case better than the protagonist and to argue for their position. We also expected that 2) viewers's leadership developmental efficacy ("LDE") (Reichard, Walker, Putter et al., 2017), would increase more for viewers than for readers, following the course. We further expected that 3) because viewing the film feels closer to lived experience than reading the case, "viewers" would be more motivated to take a C-suite leadership position (like that of the protagonist) in their future careers and would consider themselves more equipped to develop the necessary skills than "readers".

Data and method. Prior to the class students completed questionnaires measuring their leader developmental efficacy and their intentions to someday become a senior executive (Flanagan & Palmer, 2021). After reading/viewing, students filled in a questionnaire meant to assess their factual understanding of the case. At the end of the class, students completed again the LDE and the "senior executive" questionnaires. Appendix 1 describes our data and methods.

Findings and discussion. As detailed in Annex 1, hypotheses 1 and 3 were confirmed by our findings. Students who viewed the film did put themselves more into the shoes of the protagonist and were more motivated to one day become senior executives than students who read the pdf case, although the factual understanding of the case was similar between viewers and readers. However, hypothesis 2 was not confirmed, as there was no significant relationship between (changes in) students' leader developmental efficacy and whether they had watched the film or read the case. We attribute this result to the fact that students' leader developmental efficacy was on average already quite high before the experiment, leaving little room for a significant increase.

As more and more diverse audiences work with the cine-case, more insights should become available in terms of relative merits of written and cinematic cases.

Plans to further develop the initiative

We continue to add materials to the "ecosystem" that is becoming the "Clara at Crossroads Life" cine-case, such as simulation scripts, comics-style stories, quizzes. More importantly, we hope to have sparked the beginning of a new "genre" in management teaching, the cine-case, and that others will follow, thus marking a new age of the traditional management case.

References

DelCampo, R., Rogers, K., & Van Buren, H. (2010). A mockumentary as a mock experience: Using "The Office" to solidify understanding of organizational behavior topics. Journal of Organizational Behavior Education, 10(1), 1-10.

Farashahi, M., & Tajeddin, M. (2018). Effectiveness of teaching methods in business education: A comparison study on the learning outcomes of lectures, case studies and simulations. International Journal of Management Education, 16(1), 131-142.

Flanagan, D. J., & Palmer, T. B. (2021). The intentions of undergraduate business students to someday be an organization's top executive: Implications for business school leadership education. International Journal of Management Education, 19(1).

Garcia, L. D. G., & Cabanas, M. A. (2022). Teaching with the case method: opportunities and problems since the COVID-19 pivot to online. Accounting Research Journal, 35(2).

Reichard, R. J., Walker, D. O., Putter, S. E., Middleton, E., & Johnson, S. K. (2017). Believing Is Becoming: The Role of Leader Developmental Efficacy in Leader Self-Development. Journal of Leadership & Organizational Studies, 24(2), 137-156.]

Rosier, G. (2022). The case method evaluated in terms of higher education research: A pilotstudy. International Journal of Management Education, 20(3).

Yu, H. L. H., & Campbell, T. M. (2021). Teaching leadership theory with television: Useful lessons from Game of Thrones. Journal of Public Affairs Education, 27(2), 141-175.

Appendix 1. Empirical study

In order to assess the impact of the cine-case as compared to a traditional written case, we conduct a randomized experiment. We do so in the context of teaching a 6-hour synchronous online leadership development module for Post Graduate Diploma in Management students at a large business school in India. Specifically, we randomly assign students to either viewing Crossroads Life film (VIEWER=1), or to reading the corresponding PDF case (VIEWER=0), so that we can examine the impact of VIEWER on end-of-module outcomes.

At the start of the module we administer an online survey where we collect students' AGE, SEX (0=male, 1=female) and work EXPERIENCE (0=none; 1= less than a year; 2=between one and two years; 3= more than two years). In addition, we collect their responses to five Leader Developmental Efficacy items (Reichard et al., 2017) and store each student's average score (LDE). Lastly, we ask them whether they are interested in working in a corporation (CORPORATE=1) or in their own company (CORPORATE=0). For those interested in working in a corporation, we further ask to what extent, on a 7-point Likart scale, being a top executive (such as CEO or CFO) is attractive to them (C_ATTRACT); they feel they can develop the necessary skills to become such an executive (C_DEVELOP); they intend to become a top-level executive (C_INTENT); and believe they have a classmate who would some day make an excellent top level executive (C_CLASSMATE).

Over the course of the module, each student either watched "Crossroads Life" (if randomly allocated to do so, in which case VIEWER=1) or read "Clara Banu at Crossroads Life" case study (if not allocated to watch the film; in that case VIEWER=0). Students then answered a multiple-choice quiz, and the percentage score was recorded (SCORE). Moreover, they were asked to write several sentences about whether they believe they would have navigated Clara's challenges better than she did. They received one BONUS point if the quality of their argumentation stood out (regardless of the position taken). Finally, at the end of the module, they were again asked to respond to the five Leader Developmental Efficacy items, with the average value recorded as LDE_POST, as well as the four "top executive" questions, answers to which were stored as C_ATTRACT_POST, C_DEVELOP_POST, C_INTENT_POST, C_CLASSMATE_POST.

Table 1. Summary statistics

Variable	N	Mean	StdDev	Min	P25	P50	P75	Max
SEX	72	0.43	0.50	0.00	0.00	0.00	1.00	1.00
AGE	72	23.46	1.86	20.00	22.00	23.00	24.00	28.00
EXPERIENCE	72	0.50	0.93	0.00	0.00	0.00	1.00	3.00
LDE	72	6.06	0.73	4.00	5.60	6.00	6.70	7.00
CORPORATE	72	0.53	0.50	0.00	0.00	1.00	1.00	1.00
CLEVEL_ATTRACT	38	6.47	0.83	4.00	6.00	7.00	7.00	7.00
CLEVEL_INTENT	38	6.58	0.83	4.00	6.00	7.00	7.00	7.00
CLEVEL_DEVELOP	38	6.53	0.76	5.00	6.00	7.00	7.00	7.00
CLEVEL_CLASSMATE	72	5.25	1.62	1.00	4.00	5.50	7.00	7.00
VIEWER	72	0.47	0.50	0.00	0.00	0.00	1.00	1.00
SCORE	72	0.61	0.08	0.45	0.55	0.62	0.66	0.79
BONUS	72	0.08	0.28	0.00	0.00	0.00	0.00	1.00
LDE_POST	72	6.17	0.65	4.80	5.60	6.20	6.70	7.00
CLEVEL_ATTRACT_POST	72	6.33	0.92	3.00	6.00	7.00	7.00	7.00
CLEVEL_INTENT_POST	72	6.51	0.67	5.00	6.00	7.00	7.00	7.00
CLEVEL_DEVELOP_POST	72	6.47	0.67	5.00	6.00	7.00	7.00	7.00
CLEVEL_CLASSMATE_POST	72	5.49	1.45	1.00	5.00	6.00	7.00	7.00

We have full data for 72 students. Summary statistics are recorded in Table 1. Students assigned to viewing the cinematic case study as opposed to reading the corresponding text case constituted 47 percent of the group.

Table 2. Correlations

# VARIABLE	1	2	3	4	5	6	7	8	9	10	11	12	13	14	15	16	17
1 SEX	1	-0.32	-0.08	-0.05	0.04	-0.13	-0.18	-0.14	0.00	-0.09	-0.11	-0.16	-0.20	-0.29	-0.17	-0.36	-0.04
2 AGE	-0.32	1	0.54	0.05	0.10	-0.09	0.05	0.04	0.05	-0.08	0.09	0.01	0.19	0.16	0.20	0.31	0.10
3 EXPERIENCE	-0.08	0.54	1	0.17	0.00	0.13	0.10	0.14	-0.18	-0.03	0.12	0.11	0.19	0.28	0.19	0.25	0.04
4 LDE	-0.05	0.05	0.17	1	-0.02	0.78	0.56	0.60	-0.02	-0.14	0.05	0.06	0.47	0.35	0.32	0.47	0.09
5 CORP	0.04	0.10	0.00	-0.02	1				0.10	0.00	-0.11	-0.02	-0.08	0.01	-0.23	-0.08	-0.11
6 C_ATTRACT	-0.13	-0.09	0.13	0.78		1	0.65	0.66	-0.06	-0.03	-0.03	0.19	0.42	0.45	0.28	0.50	0.12
7 C_INTENT	-0.18	0.05	0.10	0.56		0.65	1	0.66	-0.18	-0.16	0.11	0.15	0.52	0.40	0.30	0.42	0.12
8 C_DEVELOP	-0.14	0.04	0.14	0.60		0.66	0.66	1	0.07	-0.17	-0.07	0.18	0.61	0.20	0.36	0.50	0.10
9 C_CLASSMATE	0.00	0.05	-0.18	-0.02	0.10	-0.06	-0.18	0.07	1	0.03	-0.09	-0.08	-0.10	-0.17	-0.12	-0.19	0.48
10 VIEWER	-0.09	-0.08	-0.03	-0.14	0.00	-0.03	-0.16	-0.17	0.03	1	0.07	0.32	-0.02	0.08	0.11	0.04	0.01
11 SCORE	-0.11	0.09	0.12	0.05	-0.11	-0.03	0.11	-0.07	-0.09	0.07	1	0.26	0.11	0.10	0.11	0.11	0.06
12 BONUS	-0.16	0.01	0.11	0.06	-0.02	0.19	0.15	0.18	-0.08	0.32	0.26	1	0.20	0.17	0.22	0.24	0.00
13 LDE_POST	-0.20	0.19	0.19	0.47	-0.08	0.42	0.52	0.61	-0.10	-0.02	0.11	0.20	1	0.43	0.54	0.52	-0.05
14 C_ATTRACT_POST	-0.29	0.16	0.28	0.35	0.01	0.45	0.40	0.20	-0.17	0.08	0.10	0.17	0.43	1	0.43	0.56	-0.02
15 C_INTENT_POST	-0.17	0.20	0.19	0.32	-0.23	0.28	0.30	0.36	-0.12	0.11	0.11	0.22	0.54	0.43	1	0.55	0.09
16 C_DEVELOP_POST	-0.36	0.31	0.25	0.47	-0.08	0.50	0.42	0.50	-0.19	0.04	0.11	0.24	0.52	0.56	0.55	1	0.05
17 C_CLASSMATE_POST	-0.04	0.10	0.04	0.09	-0.11	0.12	0.12	0.10	0.48	0.01	0.06	0.00	-0.05	-0.02	0.09	0.05	1

Correlations between the variables are presented in Table 2. We have shaded correlations in excess of 0.5 to facilitating reading of the table. We note that, as expected, AGE and EXPERIENCE are highly correlated (0.54), accordingly in our multivariate analyses we will use only AGE so as to avoid multicollinearity issues. Further, C_ATTRACT, C_DEVELOP and C_INTENT are highly correlated with each other as they capture aspects of motivation toward a C-level career; for subsequent analyses we therefore average them to form C_OVERALL variable. We do likewise with their ex-post counterpart to form C_OVERALL_POST. We note also that our C-level variables are (understandably) highly correlated with LDE, the leadership development efficacy score, so we will avoid including them in the same regression. By contrast, the correlation between LDE and PP (Promotion-Prevention), is a modest 0.13, as they quantify rather distinct notions. We also note that corresponding before and after measures (for C-level motivation and LDE) also exhibit a high degree of persistence.

Table 3. Explaining end-of-module outcomes

Dependent variable	C_OVERALL_POST	C_CLASSMATE_POST	LDE_POST	SCORE	BONUS
	(1)	(2)	(3)	(4)	(5)
SEX	-0.275	-0.040	-0.168	-0.012	-0.072
	0.155	0.903	0.258	0.582	0.299
AGE	0.088	0.017	0.054	0.003	0.000
	0.071	0.853	0.189	0.648	0.999
CORPORATE			-0.122	-0.016	-0.009
			0.384	0.415	0.885
C_OVERALL	0.367				
	0.060				
C_CLASSMATE		0.466			
		0.000			
LDE	0.131	0.264	**0.407**	0.007	0.033
	0.455	0.224	0.000	0.596	0.474
VIEWER	**0.377**	0.111	0.047	0.015	**0.175**
	0.041	0.723	0.739	0.456	0.011
Number of observations	38	72	72	72	72
Adjusted R-squared	0.379	0.219	0.217	-0.041	0.050

Our primary interest is in studying the impact of VIEWER variable on end-of-module outcomes. The results of our regressions are reported in Table 3 (where coefficient estimates are followed in italics by the associated p-values and coefficients significant at the 5 percent level are in bold; all regressions included a constant, but its coefficients are not reported for brevity). It should be noted that when C_OVERALL is measured, our sample size shrinks from 72 to 38, we will therefore only use it while examining the evolution in this specific variable – as we do in Regression 1. When we seek to explain the ex post value of this variable (which we denote in the table simply as C_OVERALL rather than C_OVERALL_POST, to save space, as there is no risk of confusion) the coefficient estimate of 0.367 for its ex ante value is close to statistical significance (p-value of 0.06), which is suggestive of persistence in this variable, as one would expect. None of the control variables (SEX, AGE, LDE) are significant. However, if the student was assigned to watch the case study rather than to read it, their motivation toward C-level responsibility increased significantly (p-value = 0.041). This is a novel result, indicating that the cinematic case format may incentivize to become more ambitious in their corporate career pursuits.

Regression 2 examines whether students' perception of their classmates' potential suitability for the C-suite (C_CLASSMATE) is affected by viewing versus reading the case. While C_CLASSMATE variable itself is highly persistent (p-value < 0.001), none of the other variables is significant, including VIEWER. The result for students own post-module Leadership Development Effectiveness self-assessment in Regression 3 is similar: while LDE itself is highly persistent (p-value < 0.001), no other variable is significant, including VIEWER.

Regression 4 examines the determinants of the students' multiple-choice quiz SCORE, which measures factual understanding of the case. None of the explanatory variables are significant, including VIEWER. This can be seen as validating that the presentation of information was well balanced between the written and cinematic versions of the case.

Lastly, regression 5 addresses the drivers of students' ability to convincingly argue about how they may have performed in place of the case's protagonist (BONUS). Given that case studies generally seek to put the student in the protagonist's shoes case study, and leadership-oriented case studies especially so, this is arguably the most important learning outcome. While none of the control variables are significant, VIEWER is, with a coefficient estimate of 0.175 and the associated p-value of 0.011.

Our takeaway from the study is as follows. Randomizing the assignment of students to viewers vs. readers facilitates causal inference. Despite its relatively small sample size, our study suggests that viewing a cinematic case facilitates students' ability to argue effectively about the case from "the shoes of the protagonist" and enhances their C-suite development self-efficacy.

Author Biography

Dr. Emilia Bunea, CFA, holds a PhD in Management from VU Amsterdam. Her research was published in Frontiers of Psychology, HBR online, London Business School Review, Les Echos, Academy of Management Proceedings. Dr. Bunea has extensive senior executive career experience, most recently as CEO of an organization with 2 million customers, as well as non-executive experience, currently as board member of an asset management company. She has been lecturing on leadership in over a dozen countries at business schools and corporate events. Her TED talk on serious leisure for leaders, delivered at London Business School, has sparked wide interest, with over a million views to date

Orchestrating Technology to Create Integrated Learning Experiences for Nursing Students

Tim Cappelli
Lead for Technology Enhanced Learning, University of Huddersfield
t.m.cappelli@hud.ac.uk

Introduction

As the UK government increases University places for student nurses, so demand for clinical placements grows. Simultaneously, hospital placements become more restricted due to Covid. To ease pressure on placements, the Nursing and Midwifery Council (NMC) have recently authorised the use of 'simulated placements' to fulfil a limited number of clinical hours. The challenge for universities is to design and deliver simulated placements that are meaningful, realistic and meet the strict criteria of the NMC. At Huddersfield University, the Department of Nursing has designed a 3-week simulated placement by orchestrating and coordinating a series of technologies to provide a structured, innovative, virtual learning experience.

This initiative was designed for the BSc Year 2 Pre-registration Nursing Programme, with a cohort of over 300 students. Whilst constraints of the curriculum demanded the 3-week simulated placement was delivered wholly online, the experience needed to replicate skills and knowledge that students would gain in a real placement, such as communication and decision making, and allow students to apply their theory of clinical practice. It was decided to focus on 'Team Building and Leadership', key skills in nursing. The objective was to encourage students to recognise and develop their role in a team and their skills in leadership. Simultaneously, being online presented an opportunity to build students' confidence in using technology. The ability to use technology is another key skill in modern nursing and although most nursing students use technology in their daily lives, many have problems translating that into using technology for studying or work (Terkes et al 2019). As educators we need to find creative ways to expose students to technology and develop their confidence. (Gonan et al, 2014).

To achieve these objectives, the team at Huddersfield developed a series of interlinked, virtual and immersive scenarios. Through smart design and careful use of technology, students were taken through a carefully scaffolded series of online activities designed to test their ability to work in teams, challenge them to take on leadership roles and build their confidence with technology.

These innovative activities were designed to be fun, engaging and motivating to encourage students to engage during the full three weeks, whilst also achieving their learning outcomes. During the placement, students completed an online Escape Room based on heart conditions, an online Murder Mystery set in a hospital, and stopped the breakout of an infection in a virtual care home. These formed the keystones of the simulated placement, together with interactive sessions on Inflammatory Bowel Disease, a group activity on promoting health and wellbeing, and a synchronous session on 'Mental Health First Aid'.

Asynchronous activities were interspersed with synchronous sessions to provide instruction and feedback, with each activity building on the last. The use of appropriate technologies also allowed instant data capture ensuring debrief sessions were relevant and targeted. Between activities, students were asked to determine their Team Role using a bespoke phone app and complete an online Action Plan.

This case describes the solution that was designed, the technologies used, the challenges that were faced, and the impact on the student experience. We believe this learning experience, and its design, has application and benefits across higher education.

Infrastructure

Initially, a working group was established to design and implement the simulated placement. Co-led by the Head of Practice Education, the Lead for Technology Enhanced Learning (TEL) and a lecturer in Clinical Skills Education, the group aimed to design the placement based on principles of good practice in simulation and in blended learning.

The literature supports the use of simulation for improving clinical skills, decision making and communication (Shephard 2010). Good practice in simulation demands problem solving, learner support, briefing and debriefing sessions, feedback and guided reflection (Kaneko and Lopes 2019). As the primary focus of this simulated placement was team building, there was also a requirement for students to work collaboratively in groups.

The design of these pedagogical elements was shaped by the commitment to blended learning and the technologies available. Cappelli and Smithies (2021) state that the success of Blended Learning is contingent on a range of interdependent organisational elements, such that curriculum design and learner support are directly related to the technological environment available. To understand the approach taken and the challenges faced, it is therefore important to understand the technological landscape.

In common with many universities, Huddersfield has an organically developed ecosystem of services that support online learning, but which are not necessarily fully integrated or holistic. Figure 1 represents this ecosystem. At its core are Brightspace, the University's VLE, and Microsoft Teams, used for all online synchronous teaching. These two systems form the backbone for online delivery.

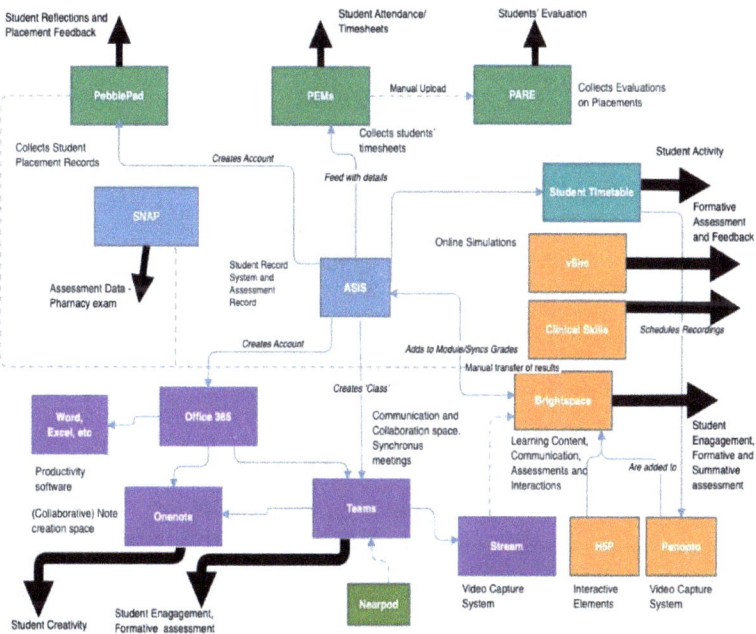

Figure 1: University Architecture

Although a good VLE, interaction in Brightspace is limited to discussion forums and basic quizzes, whilst Teams, without specialised apps, is limited to Polls and Forms. Neither provide for rich, group-based, immersive, problem-solving interactions deemed necessary for this placement. The 6-months the working group had available did not allow sufficient time to procure, test and integrate new enterprise systems into the University. Instead, the group was faced with using free-to-use or subscription-based services that would need orchestrating alongside existing systems to provide a seamless experience for students. This reflects practice at many other universities, where different technologies are often patchworked to provide interactivity in teaching. This case offers a successful example of good practice in using multiple technologies in a co-ordinated and orchestrated design, in the hope that universities can repurpose the model to their own requirements.

Since pedagogy should lead design, a series of teaching activities were designed before deciding which technologies to use. Following good practice in simulation and blended learning, the group agreed the placement should include:

- A mix of integrated asynchronous and synchronous activities
- Students working in small groups to solve problems in a series of scenarios
- Increasing levels of complexity, realism and leadership skills required with each scenario
- Application of clinical knowledge
- Application of communication and decision-making skills
- Reflection on their team role after each activity
- Peer reviews of team members' contribution to provide skills in giving feedback and help normalise their own reflections
- Active support during, and between, scenarios
- A briefing and debriefing session for each scenario
- Debriefing sessions that provided relevant feedback on students' performance
- Successful completion based on students' engagement rather than a summative assessment

Based on this, three key scenarios were agreed:

1. An Escape Room Activity where students work in groups to 'Escape' by applying clinical theory
2. A 'Murder Mystery' in which students interview suspects, find clues and work together to solve a hospital-based murder
3. An Infection Control scenario where students had to control the spread of an infection and take leadership decisions in a clinical environment.

Sub-groups were established to design each scenario, whilst the Lead for TEL and an Instructional Designer worked with each group and the wider team to ensure consistency between the scenarios. The Lead for TEL also designed the support aspects and reflection activities for students to complete between each scenario. This ensured that the reflection, support, and feedback elements of the learning journey all interlinked and built on each other to produce a meaningful, scaffolded experience.

Only then were technologies identified according to requirements. Where possible, technologies already in use, such as [H5P](H5P) and MS Forms, were used. In other cases, new technologies, such as Thinglink and Gathertown, were adopted. The choice of a particular technology often required a re-examination of the activity and how it was delivered, such that an iterative process between learning designers, academics and technologists became established, adapting and changing the design as needed. The process involved storyboarding each scenario, breaking it down to a series of content assets that were created and managed by the Lead for TEL and Instructional Designer. For example, the Murder Mystery included the creation of video interviews, made interactive using H5P and brought together in Thinglink with other clues created in Adobe Illustrator.

After 3 months, the design was completed, and the group moved into content development. The group used drama students to act as suspects in the Murder Mystery, and media students to help with filming and editing videos, ensuring students beyond Nursing benefited from the process. Each scenario was tested with both academic and IT colleagues to identify bugs and check content validity and accessibility. During this testing phase several issues were identified and addressed. In this way both reliability and validity were checked prior to release.

Figure 2 represents the workflow of learning activities students undertook, and the technologies used to produce or host the content.

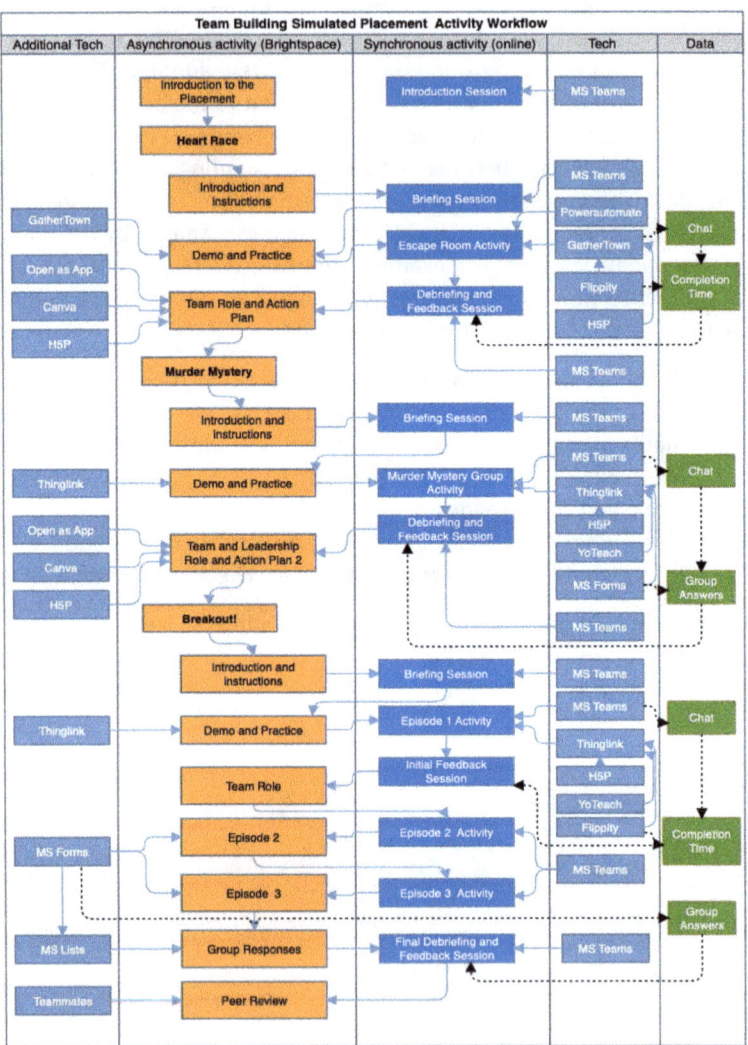

Figure 2: Activity Workflow

The workflow shows that all activities were accessed via Brightspace, supported with instruction, information, and demonstration versions of each scenario so that students could practise using the technology. This provided a structured, supported learning journey for students to complete via a familiar technology.

> Learning Outcomes

> Timetable

Three Steps to Completing the Murder Mystery!

Preparation

Before the first activity, you will have a 1 hour introduction session to brief you on what is involved and how it will work. You will then be given time to read through the preparatory material here on Brightspace. We recommend you do this once before the introductory session, in case you have any questions. This will guide you through using Thinglink and how to solve the

Find the Killer!

You will join the Teams meeting scheduled in your timetable with the rest of your group for 12.15 pm on the 1st July. Together you will enter the 'Virtual Murder Scene' using the link provided in Brightspace. You must look at the clues and interview each of the suspects. Piece together the information and discuss with your team who you think the killer is, why he was killed and how.

Reflection and Debrief

Following the Team activity you will be asked to re-visit your team role questionnaire on the app and reflect how this might have changed or be different for this activity.

There will also be a debrief session in your timetable where the lead for this activity will take you through the correct answer and the rationale.

Figure 3: Brightspace content example

The three scenarios were:

1. The Heart Race

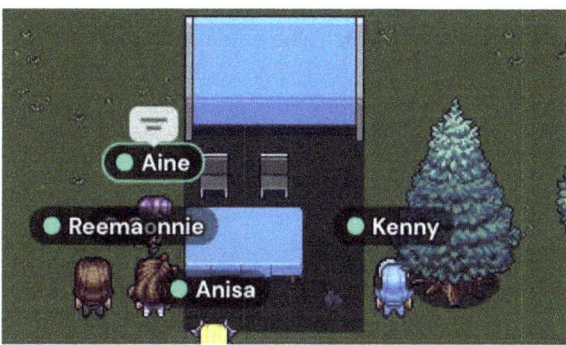

This involved each student group being placed into a custom-built space in Gathertown. This 2D immersive system allows users to create a simple avatar that can move around, interact with objects and talk to each other. As in real life, students can only hear each other when their aviators are close by. The students had to work together to solve simple problems based on their knowledge of the heart to 'escape' to a virtual Beach Bar. Gathertown was chosen as it allowed students to interact online, and for its novelty value and low adoption threshold. Being the first activity, the problem-solving and technology was kept simple, with a focus on teamwork rather than testing knowledge. Support was provided by two members of staff who could enter the room on request to help direct or guide the students.

2. Murder Mystery

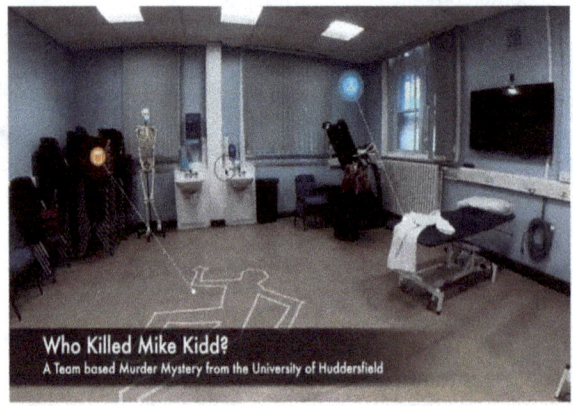

The student groups were timetabled to meet in MS Teams and asked to work through this hospital-based murder mystery built in Thinglink. The scenario consisted of a series of 360° rooms that students could explore independently. Each room contained clues, and a suspect who could be interviewed using interactive videos built in H5P. The students had to allocate tasks, exchange information, and decide on the murderer before submitting their answer via a single MS Form for the group. Support was provided via a live chat room in YoTeach staffed by two members of the team.

3. Breakout!

Once again, the student groups were timetabled to meet in MS Teams to complete a scenario created in Thinglink. The scenario was based in a Care Home where the group needed to prevent the outbreak of an unknown infection. Students had to apply their knowledge of Infection Control and make leadership decisions in a time-limited environment. This was chosen as the last scenario as it was the most complex and true-to-life; the two previous scenarios providing students with the confidence to tackle it successfully. This scenario continued over two days as students were given updates on the escalating infection. As the infection grew, they had to make decisions on the wellbeing and safety of residents and staff.

Each of the three scenarios was preceded with an online briefing session, to ensure students understood the task, and followed with a debrief session to provide feedback and generate discussion. Because the technologies included a range of data capturing systems, it was possible to quickly download information from each activity and include it in the debrief presentation. For example, Flippity captured the response time for each group, whilst MS Forms captured the groups' Murder Mystery answers (figure 4). In addition, MS Teams' Attendance Report provided an instant record of each student's attendance.

Figure 4: Activity Feedback

Between each scenario, students were asked to download and use a bespoke phone app built using Open-as-App. (Figure 5).

They used this to identify their predominate Team Role and then, using an infographic built in Canva (Figure 6) and a document template built in H5P, they completed a structured Action Plan on how to improve their contribution to the team. The students could download and save this as a PDF and submit it as evidence of successful completion of the task. Students were also encouraged to add the Action Plan to their professional portfolio and discuss it with their Academic Advisors.

Figure 5: Team Role app instructions

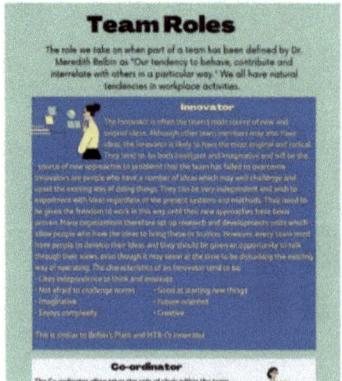

Figure 6: Team Role Infographic and Action Plan in Brightspace

After the second scenario, students were also asked to identify their Leadership Style based on the American Association of Nurse Assessment Coordination (AANAC) Leadership model and how they might apply this to the final activity.

Following the final scenario, each student received an email from [Teammates](https://shorturl.at/dyz39) asking them to provide feedback on each of their fellow team members. After being moderated, this was automatically collated, anonymised, and returned to the relevant students by Teammates. This allowed students to see how others saw their role in the team and to reflect further on this feedback.

See more at https://shorturl.at/dyz39

Challenges

The main challenges were known beforehand and planned for as part of the design. For example, the group were aware of the limitations of Brightspace and Teams in providing story-based, immersive experiences. To overcome this, a close working relationship between academics, instructional designers and the Lead for TEL was formed to determine requirements and identify suitable cloud-based, subscription services that could fulfil these requirements quickly and easily. Existing tools, such as H5P, Flippity and MS Forms, were used to create activities within these main platforms. This risked overloading students with different technologies. To avoid this, technologies were 'hidden' as part of the wider scenario. For example, the H5P questions and MS Forms were embedded into Thinglink or Gathertown, so students simply completed these as part of the scenario; the YoTeach chat room was accessed from a link in Thinglink, so students were unaware of using a different technology. Where students needed to interface with new technology, they were provided with instructional videos, support and the chance to practise before each scenario. Using technology was also built into the learning outcomes of the placement. By introducing different technologies, scaffolding the support, and making the activity 'fun', the aim was to build students' confidence with technology as the placement progressed. As such, the 'challenge' become part of the learning.

Another challenge was how to support students through a 3-week placement that was wholly online. The issue of supporting remote students is well documented (Crawley 2012). One approach is the creation of an online learning community (LaPointe & Reisetter 2008). Fortunately, the Nursing Department had established and maintained a Learning Community for Nursing Students in MS Teams. The group utilised this by creating a dedicated channel for the simulated placement in the community (figure 7). Students could use this to post questions that were quickly answered by tutors or fellow students. Support during the scenarios was provided through live chat, staffed by two members of staff, allowing quick resolution of issues.

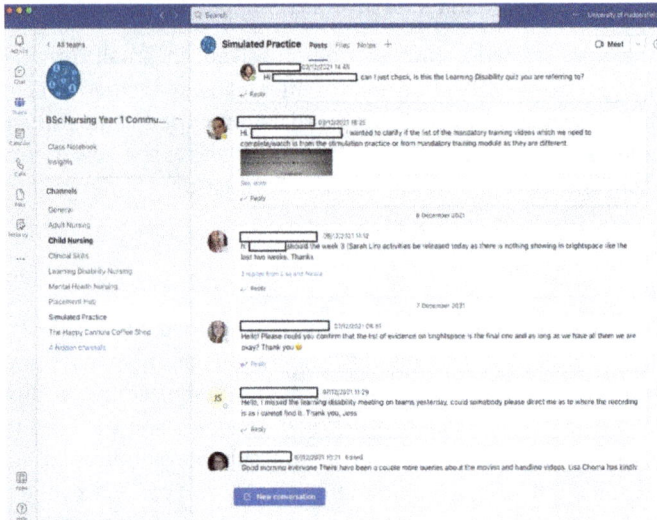

Figure 7: Learning Community

An unexpected challenge arose when planning the Escape Rooms. The free version of Gathertown is limited to 25 users per space. There were over 300 students on the placement. To overcome this, students were allocated discrete timeslots over a two-day period and emails with links and passwords were sent at timed intervals using MS Powerautomate. This freed up staff from focussing on processing students to instead focus on support.

How the Initiative was Received

Student satisfaction with the placement was measured as part of an overall Evaluation plan that draws on the Kirkpatrick Evaluation Model (Kirkpatrick 1975) as well as Bowyer and Chambers' framework for evaluating blended learning (Bowyer and Chambers 2017).

A series of evaluation metrics were identified and data collected through a combination of student questionnaires and interrogation of data from the systems. This showed the initiative was particularly well received by students. Scoring each activity against six statements, 80% or more of the students agreed or strongly agreed with every statement, with most scoring over 90% agreement (Figure 8). This demonstrates their satisfaction with the scenarios and the effectiveness of the learning.

1. How much do you agree/disagree with these statements about The Heart Race (0 point)

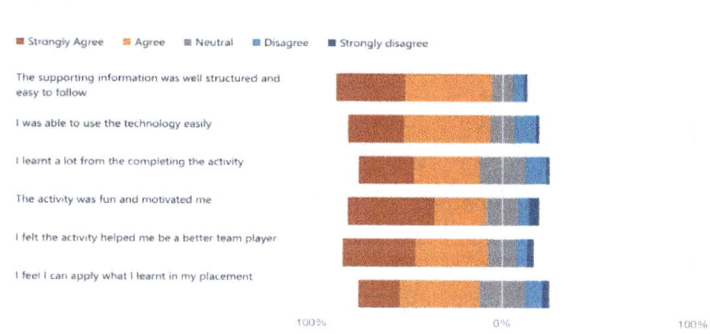

3. How much do you agree/disagree with these statements about The Murder Mystery (0 point)

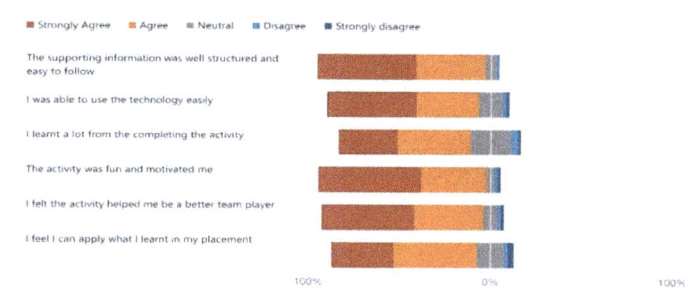

7. How much do you agree/disagree with these statements about The Infection Control Activity (0 point)

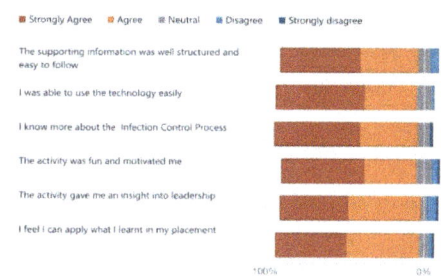

Figure 8: Student feedback

Their comments on the evaluation form reinforced this.

> "Made us all work well within the team to get the answers and unlock the padlocks. Information provided about the heart was good"

> "The murder mystery was my favourite activity of the placement as it was engaging and got our minds working. It helped some of the team members open up and become more comfortable as-well. Great activity."

> "loved this actively, was perfect for me as I am a visual learner and enjoy working out puzzles etc, I am also dyslexia so the fact you are doing things like this that work well with my dyslexia mind and allow me to show my strengths is amazing thank you so much :)"

> "This was probably the most difficult activity of the lot. However that did not stop it from being fun and engaging. Making decisions in part two and three was very difficult and allowed us to put ourselves in the shoes of the ward manager etc, which was great and insightful."

The placement has now been delivered twice more since its inception, and each time the evaluation results have reflected similarly high levels of student satisfaction.

In addition to the evaluation form, staff noticed students were fully engaging during the activities and were motivated to complete them; often difficult to achieve with online learning. The chat in Gathertown and Teams was particularly active during the scenarios, with students voicing their theories. Figure 9 demonstrates this.

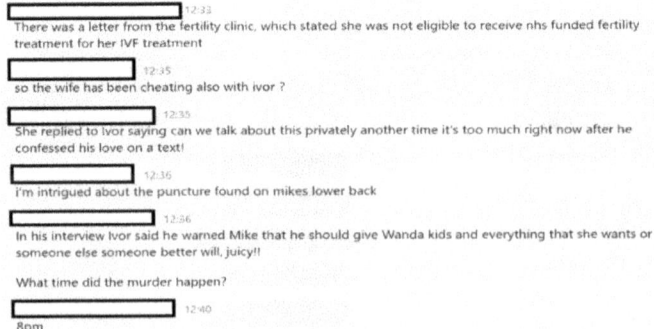

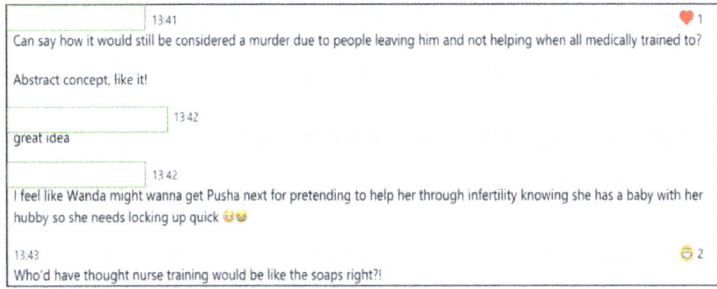

Figure 9: Chat screenshots

This was also reflected during the debrief sessions which directly followed each scenario. Students were keen to voice their theories, but also express how much they had enjoyed each of the activities and what they had learned from it.

The Learning Outcomes

The Placement had two key learning outcomes:

- Collaborate via a virtual environment with other health care professional students to build on your leadership and team working skills.
- Reflect upon leadership styles and group dynamics when working in teams from your own and colleague perspectives

These set out to address the NMC Standards of proficiency, Platform 5, "Leading and managing nursing care and working in teams" whilst also building students' confidence in using technology to collaborate.

Improvements in leadership and teamwork are difficult to measure objectively over a short period, but the evaluation plan described above sought to gauge students' own measure of the effectiveness of the learning.

For example, the statement, "I felt the activity helped me be a better team player" was scored as strongly agree/agree by over 85% of students for all activities, whilst 90% of students strongly agreed/agreed with the statement, "the activity gave me an insight into leadership" for the Breakout Scenario.

In addition, comments from students in the evaluation indicate that students were reflecting and understanding their own role in a team successfully.

> "It was fun and didn't feel like work, however raised my awareness around teamwork and leadership skills"

> "This was good for team working and taking on different roles working together to get one outcome everyone was happy with"

> "I enjoyed this activity and it did push me out of my comfort zone in terms of pushing my leadership skills forward when others don't speak out."

> "One of the best activities, we spilt in groups and merged together at the end to discuss the outcome and complete the activity"

There was further evidence of this when students were asked to identify their peer's contribution on Teammates. These demonstrated a real understanding of different team roles.

> "[student A] played a really important part of our team by being a supporter. She was really good in ensuring everyone within the team was included and ensured everyone got their points and opinions across. She always reassured and praised other team members. She helped to encourage and motivate us as a team. "

> "[student B] contributed quite a lot to the groupwork. She shared her ideas, experiences and knowledge with the team and during the activities she frequently thought outside of the box, which was a great way of exploring and learning new ideas for me and maybe for other students too."

Although focussed on team-building, leadership skills and improving their confidence with technology, it's important to recognise the value of these placements in the application of clinical theory, replicating what students would be asked to do in a real placement. Once again student feedback demonstrates this:

> "Well structured and great support from teachers. I learn lot about infection control process on workplace."

> "Helped me to learn more about infection control process, and motivated me more to research about infection control process."

> "The Heart Race was a good interesting group activity. I got so many (sic) information about the heart through this scenario activity."

Plans to Further Develop the Initiative

Following the successful first delivery of this placement in February 2022, the Department of Nursing have pursued a 4-step approach to develop the initiative further. These are:

1. Improve the initiative using feedback from students and staff.

Since its initial delivery, the initiative has been delivered twice in its original format, and on each occasion the comments and feedback from students during the debrief sessions was used to further improve the validity and reliability of the content. The evaluation comments have also been analysed and used to improve both the content and the organisation of the scenarios; for example, based on student feedback, students now have the opportunity to meet in their teams prior to the first activity. This allows them to get to know each other and plan their approach. The learning continues to receive student satisfaction ratings as good as, or better, than the first implementation.

2. Repurpose the content for different programmes

Members of the design team, drawn from across the Department, were quick to recognise the potential of these scenarios in their own specialisms. As such, some of the individual scenarios have been used as stand-alone learning activities in different parts of the department. For example, the Murder Mystery has been used in the simulated placements for year 3 students, demonstrating both the transferability and adaptability of the initiative.

3. Reproduce the design principles in other disciplines

In addition to re-using the content in other areas of nursing, the team were keen to share the content and its design across the University in the belief that similar approaches could be adopted in other areas of the curriculum and other disciplines. For example, the lessons and good practices learnt from this initiative have already been transferred to the design of simulated placements for years' one and three of the nursing programme. The smart design and use of multiple technologies adopted in these years has provided a consistent, high-standard learning experience for students. To spread the initiative further, the team have delivered a workshop on how to create similar immersive, interactive scenarios at the University's Teaching and Learning Conference. This was extremely well received has led directly to several other departments, such as psychology, creating their own version of the Escape Room scenario, again demonstrating the transferability of this approach. There are plans to repeat the workshop within the University with the Lead for TEL and Instructional Designer providing specialised support to new initiatives.

4. Disseminate the approach to the learning community

Although similar immersive scenarios such as this have been used in Medical Education (Gillaspy 2021) they have not been sequenced together in this manner to provide a complete online learning solution that characterises this novel approach. The hope is to develop the approach and the initiative further and to promulgate good practice in the application of multiple technologies to build a scaffolded series of scenarios across Higher Education and beyond. To this end, the team have secured a workshop at a National Learning Conference in September 2022 to demonstrate the principles and approach.

Through such workshops we hope to provide others with the tools and knowledge to create similar activities, transferring these practices to other disciplines and applications of simulation.

The issue of placement shortages and the need to provide learning-rich simulations is not restricted to Huddersfield or to Nursing. This initiative demonstrates it is possible to use widely available, inexpensive technologies to create learning that meets good practice standards in simulation and in blended learning, notably to:

- pose problems that required student collaboration and application of knowledge
- provide situational and extraneous support
- provide contextualised and timely briefing and debriefing sessions
- provide instant and targeted feedback
- allow guided reflection
- provide a mix of interlinked synchronous and asynchronous activities

However, for some universities, the need is more immediate, and Huddersfield have agreed to sell the simulated placement as a complete learning event to at least one university. Huddersfield hope to develop this opportunity further by providing content and consultancy where it is required, thereby helping to build good practice in the sector.

References

Bowyer, J. and Chambers, L., 2017. Evaluating blended learning: Bringing the elements together. *Research Matters: A Cambridge Assessment Publication*, *23*(1), pp.17-26.

Cappelli, T. and Smithies, A., 2021, October. Building Organisational Capacity for Blended Learning: An Evidence-Based Approach. In *20th European Conference on e-Learning, ECEL 2021* (pp. 73-79).

Crawley, A., 2012. *Supporting online students: A practical guide to planning, implementing, and evaluating services*. John Wiley & Sons.

Gillaspy, E., 2021. Suffering from lecture lethargy? Break free and create an escape room. https://ccl.uclan.ac.uk/2021/08/19/suffering-from-lecture-lethargy-break-free-and-create-an-escape-room/

Gonen, A., Sharon, D., Offir, A. and Lev-Ari, L., 2014. How to enhance nursing students' intention to use information technology: the first step before integrating it in nursing curriculum. *CIN: Computers, Informatics, Nursing*, *32*(6), pp.286-293.

Kaneko, R.M.U. and Lopes, M.H.B.D.M., 2019. Realistic health care simulation scenario: what is relevant for its design?. *Revista da Escola de Enfermagem da USP*, *53*.

Kirkpatrick, D.L., 1975. Techniques for evaluating training programs. *Evaluating training programs*, pp.1-17.

LaPointe, L. and Reisetter, M., 2008. Belonging online: Students' perceptions of the value and efficacy of an online learning community. *International Journal on E-learning*, 7(4), pp.641-665.

Shepherd, C.K., McCunnis, M., Brown, L. and Hair, M., 2010. Investigating the use of simulation as a teaching strategy. *Nursing Standard*, 24(35).

Terkes, N., Celik, F., & Bektas, H. (2019). Determination of nursing students' attitudes towards the use of technology. *Japan Journal of Nursing Science*, 16(1), 17-24.

Acknowledgements

This initiative was designed and developed by a dedicated team at the University of Huddersfield and the author acknowledges Linda Sanderson and Lisa Choma in the development and organisation of the simulated placement; Karen Currall in the development and writing of the murder mystery; Mathew Blears and Sharon Hunter in creating the Infection Control Scenario and finally Hayley Hewitt as Instructional Designer and learning technologist.

Author Biography

Tim Cappelli has worked with learning technology for over 20 years, from setting up work-based learning centres to introducing blended learning initiatives to HE. He managed the first large-scale deployment of iPads in HE, the development of a learning platform in WordPress and the creation of a digital Curriculum Mapping Tool.

A Novel Converged Learning Model as an Agile Method for Teaching and Learning Before, During, and After the Pandemic

Fadi P. Deek and Regina Collins
New Jersey Institute of Technology, USA
fadi.deek@njit.edu, regina.s.collins@njit.edu

Abstract: In 2013, New Jersey Institute of Technology (NJIT) proposed an integrated digital learning model to achieve functional convergence of the physical and virtual campus in a learning environment in which students have the opportunity to engage in a course either remotely or in a classroom environment, by choice and alternating the mode to fit their needs, with technology blurring the distinction between the two environments. This model was used at NJIT for select courses until the COVID-19 pandemic. Having proven successful on a small scale, the converged learning model was expanded, by necessity, to most freshman and sophomore level classes in Fall 2020, with junior, senior, and graduate level courses added in Spring 2021. Through this model, social distance could be maintained by inviting only some of the students to physically attend each class session while others joined remotely, alternating invitations to allow all students the opportunity to attend class in person and enabling our university to remain open essentially throughout the pandemic. Surveys captured student and faculty perceptions of the technology and the mode of learning and informed adjustments, and course evaluations assessed students' perceptions of learning in the modality. Results suggest that the rapid expansion of converged learning initially challenged both students and faculty, but by the second semester, because of strategic planning and investments, every measured outcome showed improvement. This has given us confidence to expand our investments in this modality in alignment with our strategic vision of a global campus. We share, through this case study, how our converged learning model formed the basis for NJIT's *Pandemic Recovery Plan* and describe how our mission, while ensuring the safety and well-being of our campus community, endured.

Introduction

New Jersey Institute of Technology (NJIT) is the public polytechnic research university of the state of New Jersey. Founded in 1881 as the Newark Technical School, NJIT is now classified as a Carnegie Doctoral Very High Research (R1) university comprising six academic colleges. The College of Science and Liberal Arts (CSLA), the Hillier College of Architecture and Design (HCAD), the Martin Tuchman School of Management (MTSM), the Newark College of Engineering (NCE), and the

Ying Wu College of Computing (YWCC) award undergraduate, master's, and doctoral degrees as well as post-baccalaureate certificates. The Albert Dorman Honors College offers a more enriching experience for undergraduate students majoring in any of the university's academic disciplines.

NJIT has a history of deploying digital tools in support of all modes of instruction and in all disciplines (Deek, Deek, & Friedman, 1999). In fact, in the 1980s NJIT earned a reputation as a visionary leader in online education for its pioneering work on the virtual classroom and asynchronous learning (Hiltz, 1986). In 2013, academic leadership at the New Jersey Institute of Technology (NJIT) proposed a new concept of *Convergence–A Vision and Framework for Leadership in Digital Learning* (Office of the Provost, 2013). This educational vision outlined a new modality in which "the physical classroom and the virtual classroom will asymptotically converge." Through specialized technology, remote learners and those physically present in the classroom would participate in the same course section in real time regardless of location, thereby creating a "converged learning" environment.

The objective of this new model was to create an *anywhere* classroom in which a student would have the opportunity to transparently engage in learning regardless of location, with both modalities occurring in the same course section. Because of individual circumstances, one mode might have advantages for a given student at a given time, but the tools and venues open to all students would provide equivalent outcomes, thereby ensuring equity and access. This synergy also extends to university resources. Because converged learning students could, for each class session, choose to attend by coming to the classroom, logging into the class from their dorms or nearby apartments, or joining the class from another state or country, admission, registration procedures, and costs would be the same. Students participating in converged learning would have access to all campus and university resources and would be treated the same as traditional (face-to-face) students.

In addition, academic standards would be consistent because course content and learning outcomes would stand independent of delivery mode. Those attending class in-person would experience the delivery of the course content as they would in a traditional class—except that they would be joined via synchronous streaming by other students taking the course from a distance, anywhere in the world. These remote students would be held to the same standards for academic excellence as their classmates on campus: they would engage in the same discussions, do the same homework, and take the same exams. In this way, the classroom would be brought to the remote learner in real time, and he or she would participate in the class in the same way as those physically present.

The converged learning initiative was integrated into NJIT's *2020 Vision* strategic plan (Office of the Provost, 2015) which established an ambitious set of strategic goals and objectives for the university to achieve by 2020. For converged learning, the objective was to provide a more inclusive learning environment that would allow students to attend class regardless of their location or situation while at the same time reclaiming NJIT's leadership in digital learning that it held more than a quarter century ago. To this end, the converged modality was launched in Spring 2016 for a small number of courses in specially equipped classrooms. The significant cost of investment in instructional technology required for the converged learning model was a factor in instituting a steady but cautious approach to adoption and expansion. As a result, a comprehensive assessment of the learning model and its outcomes was not initially feasible, although converged courses were included in all routine assessments of learning outcomes conducted at the university. Recent circumstances have changed both of these situations.

In Spring 2020, like the rest of the higher education enterprise and the rest of the world for that matter, the global pandemic forced NJIT to move to remote operations, including instruction, research, and business functions. Our deliberate investments in instructional technology and increased digital capabilities across our campus, accelerated in the period immediately after the start of the pandemic, proved both wise and timely. In March of 2020, NJIT instantaneously and seamlessly shifted to converged learning in which instructors taught synchronously using their home computers with students joining regardless of location. This remote converged format worked remarkably well given its sudden implementation. With a minimum of equipment (laptop, microphone, and camera), instructors were teaching and interacting with their students ten days after the official move to remote operations. For instructors and students lacking the necessary technologies, the university provided devices to facilitate the sudden transition to remote converged learning.

At the same time, guided by a comprehensive *Pandemic Recovery Plan* (Office of the Provost, 2020), the university began to prepare for a return to campus by the Fall of that year, using converged learning as a means to support appropriate social distancing while still providing students with on-campus, face-to-face experiences. The converged format provided a flexibility that was well suited to the uncertainty caused by the pandemic. First, it allowed students to determine their preferred method of attendance: for those students anxious to return to (or come to) campus, converged learning provided the option to attend class in person or join from the library, residence halls, or other study spaces made available by the university; for students (or families) concerned about returning too soon, remote attendance was available but with the ever-present option to choose to attend in person.

In the Fall of 2020, 42% of all academic courses were offered in the converged modality, with priority given to freshmen and sophomore-level classes to ensure these students built a connection to the NJIT community through face-to-face experiences. Labs were also offered in the converged modality with students alternating in-person attendance in order to gain the practical experience necessary for lab work. In Spring 2021, 34% of courses were offered in the converged modality, including upper level undergraduate classes and graduate-level classes. A breakdown of converged course sections by college is shown in Table 1.

Table 1. Converged Course Section Frequency Distribution across Colleges/Schools

College	Fall 2020		Spring 2021	
	n	%	n	%
College of Science and Liberal Arts (CSLA)	426	61.4%	220	35.7%
Hillier College of Architecture and Design (HCAD)	34	37.0%	33	35.5%
Martin Tuchman School of Management (MTSM)	40	32.3%	33	27.0%
Newark College of Engineering (NCE)	169	33.3%	207	41.6%
Ying Wu College of Computing (YWCC)	92	26.3%	81	23.9%

A robust set of course sections were offered by all NJIT colleges and schools in the converged modality, with significant participation by the College of Science and Liberal Arts. This is attributed to their dual role at the university in that they offer their own degree programs but are also responsible for a large component of the lower-level undergraduate general education requirements (GER) including courses in mathematics, physics, chemistry, social sciences, and first-year writing. As early as the second semester of their first year, students in many of our disciplines also begin to take courses in their major, leading to a more balanced distribution of converged courses between all the schools and colleges by the Spring 2021 semester.

The Infrastructure

The expansion of the converged learning model required a substantial investment in technology as well as training of faculty. In January of 2020, NJIT had 11 classrooms equipped with built-in sophisticated video conferencing systems to facilitate converged teaching and learning. By fall of that year, 17 additional classrooms (spread throughout six buildings on campus) had been equipped with built-in systems. An additional 109 mobile carts with unified intelligent 360° camera/microphone/speaker video conferencing technology were purchased and distributed across academic spaces.

At the same time, the university's instructional designers worked with faculty to adapt their courses to the converged modality, and a classroom with a built-in video conferencing system was made available for faculty to become acquainted with the technology prior to the start of the semester. Members of the Office of Digital Learning were on call to troubleshoot problems.

The converged learning modality allowed shifts to the appropriate degree of social distancing by setting a maximum number of face-to-face students allowed in each class. Students were split into groups that alternated in-class attendance so that there were never more than 33% or 50% of enrolled students in a classroom at the same time. To manage classroom attendance, an app with AI capabilities was implemented prior to the start of the Fall 2020 semester. This app offered classroom seats to a subset of enrolled students on a rotating basis, essentially providing students who wished to converge physically a chance to be in the classroom within a certain time cycle. Students who accepted the invitation to attend class in person that day were guaranteed a seat that was appropriately distanced from other students in attendance. If a student declined the invitation to attend in person, that seat was offered to another student, with preference given to students who had not physically attended class recently.

The Challenges

The rapid expansion of converged learning raised concerns about the quality of teaching and learning in this modality. To address these concerns, and seizing the opportunity to finally conduct a wide-scale assessment of the model, surveys were distributed in the Fall and Spring semesters to assess student and faculty satisfaction with the converged learning and teaching experience and to identify any issues requiring immediate attention. One issue that was identified was difficulty for remote students in hearing the instructors in classrooms equipped with the mobile carts, with only 44% of students rating the quality of the audio as excellent or good. To address this problem, clip-on microphones were provided to faculty, resulting in a 17% increase in excellent and good ratings (61%) of audio by the spring of 2021. Additional technologies were also provided, including document cameras in courses where faculty demonstrated how to solve complex equations.

Interactions between students were also found to be a challenge in Fall 2020, with only 27% of students stating that opportunities to interact with classmates were excellent or good. Additional faculty training for the converged modality, as well as modifications to video conferencing technologies such as breakout rooms, led to more positive perceptions regarding opportunities for interaction by the spring of 2021, with 32% of students rating the opportunities as excellent or good. Similarly, in Fall 2020, 29% of students rated their ability to stay connected with classmates as excellent or good, increasing to 36% in Spring 2021.

Training, technological support, and the experiences of the fall semester all served to substantially improve the student learning experience for Spring 2021. The support provided by the Office of Digital Learning and the university's instructional designers resulted in a 16% increase in students' perceptions regarding their instructors' mastery of the course delivery software, with 42% of students rating this as good or excellent in Fall 2020 compared to 58% in Spring 2021. Students also felt more confident in their own skills with remote learning technology, with excellent and above average ratings increasing from 56% (Fall 2020) to 63% (Spring 2021).

How the Initiative Was Received

Overall, the converged learning model had some compelling benefits. Particularly during the pandemic, students wishing to have on-campus interactions were still able to do so, while students concerned about coming to campus were able to continue their education by joining converged courses virtually. The converged model also facilitated the development of contingency plans should any change (increase or decrease) in social distancing be mandated. For example, if the semester began fully remote, the easing of restrictions could be accommodated seamlessly by increasing in-person presence through the converged modality.

In addition to the surveys conducted during the Fall 2020 and Spring 2021 semesters to identify issues and capture student satisfaction with the converged learning experience, course evaluations were conducted at the end of each of these semesters. As with the converged learning surveys, notable improvements were evidenced between Fall 2020 and Spring 2021 regarding students' perceptions of the educational value of the course, the instructor's ability to communicate the course content and their encouragement of class participation, and the overall teaching effectiveness of the instructor in the converged modality. Because the courses in each college are very different (some are intensive 6-hour studios while others are labs or lectures and recitations), students' perceptions of converged courses are summarized by college in Table 2 below. These responses reflect the results of the converged learning surveys: namely that teaching and learning had improved in the converged modality by the Spring 2021 semester.

The results shown in Table 2 indicate that every measure appreciated between Fall 2020 and Spring 2021, with some measures showing significant improvement. The overall teaching effectiveness of the instructor increased substantially, by nearly 0.5 in certain colleges, suggesting instructors' increasing adaptation and comfort level with the initially unfamiliar modality. This improvement was particularly important for our university because this measure is indicative of quality instruction and, in fact, is used in a number of ways including merit salary increases and promotions. However, improvements were not consistent across all colleges and schools; the smaller increase for this measure in NCE could be attributed to the difficulty, compared to other subjects, of conveying engineering content remotely and digitally.

Table 2. Means of Student Course Evaluation Responses by College/School

College/Course Evaluation Survey Statement	Fall 2020	Spring 2021
CSLA		
Overall educational value of course	2.87	3.09
Instructor's ability to communicate the course content	3.04	3.26
Instructor's encouragement of active class participation	3.04	3.24
Overall teaching effectiveness of the instructor	2.99	3.24
HCAD		
Overall educational value of course	3.05	3.41
Instructor's ability to communicate the course content	3.05	3.52
Instructor's encouragement of active class participation	3.13	3.47
Overall teaching effectiveness of the instructor	3.01	3.48
MTSM		
Overall educational value of course	3.00	3.32

College/Course Evaluation Survey Statement	Fall 2020	Spring 2021
Instructor's ability to communicate the course content	3.11	3.52
Instructor's encouragement of active class participation	3.04	3.24
Overall teaching effectiveness of the instructor	3.06	3.45
NCE		
Overall educational value of course	3.05	3.11
Instructor's ability to communicate the course content	3.08	3.13
Instructor's encouragement of active class participation	3.02	3.11
Overall teaching effectiveness of the instructor	3.03	3.05
YWCC		
Overall educational value of course	2.63	3.07
Instructor's ability to communicate the course content	2.62	3.12
Instructor's encouragement of active class participation	2.57	3.11
Overall teaching effectiveness of the instructor	2.58	3.07

In the past, many more courses in computing, humanities, and management had typically been offered in the converged modality. Because of this, NCE faculty had less experience teaching in this delivery mode. In fact, the engineering labs were the most difficult courses to deliver in the converged mode during the first semester. To address this, academic departments were very proactive in producing video content of laboratory experiments that was made available to students who chose to attend virtually or where space constraints limited the number of students who could attend physically. Interviews with students suggest that many other students also opted to use the videos to reinforce what they learned regardless of the modality. By the Spring 2021 semester, lab instruction and virtual student participation improved as the university had adequate time to identify software simulations to replace our rudimentary videos.

One major concern for faculty was the challenge of actively engaging students whose lives, like everyone else's, were abruptly disrupted in so many ways. However, an encouraging observation is that the largest gain made between the fall and spring semesters in three of the five colleges/schools (HCAD, NCE, and YWCC), was in the measure of the instructor's encouragement of active class participation. Having themselves identified this as a concern in the Fall semester, instructors were able to significantly increase students' perceptions of engagement. This was a deliberate and conscious effort, but results suggest that. MTSM and CSLA did not realize as significant an increase in that measure. This may be because instructors in these schools were already more skilled in engaging remote students through a variety of modalities.

The instructor's ability to communicate the course content also increased between Fall 2020 and Spring 2021, resulting in a corresponding increase in students' perception of the overall educational value of the course. In fact, of all the measures listed, the educational value of the course experienced the most substantial gain across all colleges.

The Learning Outcomes

The rapid expansion of NJIT's converged learning format initially led to some "growing pains" as instructors and students adjusted to a blended classroom in which they could interact with the person sitting next to them or located hundreds of miles away. These challenges are reflected in the Fall 2020 converged learning survey and course evaluation results. Yet the increases in satisfaction with the converged learning experience and in the end-of-semester course evaluations by Spring 2021 suggest that once instructors and students acclimated to the new modality and worked through the technological issues, converged learning was a successful method for delivering a quality educational experience. In other words, despite the challenges, this experience proved that converged learning is a flexible and inclusive modality that allows learners to determine their preferred method of attending class on any given day while still sharing a common educational experience. Moreover, NJIT now has a proven approach to continue instructional delivery to our students even when physical disruptions occur.

Our large-scale implementation of the converged learning model also evidenced the necessity for all students and instructors to have access to the Internet as well as a suite of reliable computing and communication tools (UNESCO, 2020). As a polytechnic university, NJIT was able to quickly meet the needs of students and faculty. However, technology by itself has never been and will never be the sole enabler of learning. In other words, providing video conferencing technology is not equal to teaching. NJIT has recently created the Office of Online Programs which now oversees the expansion of our Digital Learning and Instructional Design efforts. The goal is to continue to work with academic departments to examine and enhance pedagogy related to delivering remote instruction digitally, placing the emphasis on the content and its quality.

Another focus is to strengthen the connections between the different communities of students (traditional, remote, and mixed modal) and between these students and their instructors. A technology-rich learning environment will facilitate opportunities to interact through the application of emerging tools and devices, and analytics will provide feedback on student engagement and interactions. Analytics and artificial intelligence will be used to personalize the learning experiences of individuals to suit their abilities and needs while also giving instructors better understanding of students' learning styles. The STEM nature of our disciplines will also benefit from the adoption of augmented reality by bringing abstractions closer to reality, especially for lab-based courses.

Plans to Further Develop the Initiative

NJIT's transformational strategic plan, *2020 Vision*, resulted in significant improvements in student outcomes, tremendous growth in externally funded research, and substantial investments in classroom infrastructure. The university recently launched another ambitious plan, *Building on a Strong Foundation–NJIT 2025*. This plan, now in its third year, focuses on five different priorities: Students, Faculty, Research, Resources, and Prominence. An objective that crosscuts all of these priorities is the development of a virtual, global campus which will offer undergraduate and graduate programs using innovative remote delivery modalities as well as through development of physical presences beyond our Newark campus. In addition to increasing accessibility of programs to populations with time restrictions or limited access to higher education, NJIT Global will expand our international visibility as we grow beyond the limits of our current physical infrastructure in the City of Newark. This is consistent with our broad vision "to be a preeminent public polytechnic research university with local and global impact." Specifically, our strategic plan makes a clear statement that we will do this by "transforming ourselves into a global campus that innovates pedagogy and technology to advance our mission around the world." Converged learning is a cornerstone of this initiative.

The acceleration of investment in the infrastructure necessary to support converged learning during the pandemic resulted in our five-year *2020 Vision* strategic goal being completed in one year. Moving forward, NJIT plans to expand the converged modality to exciting new opportunities including the establishment of NJIT Global. With converged learning as a central feature, NJIT Global will allow our on-campus students and students from other countries to attend class together, with instruction occurring here or there. Even while we build facilities overseas, converged learning allows us to commingle our student populations and benefit from instructional assets at any location.

Finally, as new generations of students make their way into college classrooms, many of whom have grown up in a technologically connected world, they are demanding flexibility in their learning experience. That same flexibility is also important to non-traditional learners. What is common, however, is that all students at all levels of education have experienced a significant learning deficit as a result of sudden transition to remote learning and other serious ramifications of the pandemic. This is even more pronounced among students from disadvantaged communities who may not be as well equipped upon entering institutions of higher education. However, a recent study suggests that children raised in communities with more "economic connectedness (cross-class interactions)" are much more likely to improve their own socio-economic status, suggesting the importance of building connections among a diverse population of students (Opportunity Insights, 2022). Converged learning makes this a reality by offering a true blended community that mitigates socio-economic barriers (U.S. Department of Education, 2021).

Conclusion

The value proposition of higher education has been under scrutiny for some time but, despite this, reform is at best nascent. While there are clearly compelling reasons for continuing to teach and learn in traditional classrooms, it is just as clear that other modes of digital delivery have their own compelling rationales. As higher education institutions resume their strategic planning in a post-pandemic world, it is important to reflect on their recent experiences and incorporate the knowledge they acquired in order to successfully effect a necessary redesign of their learning spaces and the communities they enable.

For NJIT, converged learning is a first step in transforming how we deliver a quality educational experience to diverse learners with the flexibility to "meet them where they are." Our success in delivering emergency remote learning reflects the deliberate creation of a flexible pedagogy and investment in technology at NJIT. Our experiences, thus, direct us to prepare for a future in higher education that seamlessly mixes face-to-face and online, which is also different from the various forms of hybrid learning.

To be clear, no one is urging the total dismantling of the physical infrastructure for teaching and learning. Similarly, no one is asserting that the massive and fast-moving migration toward online education will ease once we are fully beyond the current pandemic. Thus, aligning learning theories and practices with an enabling digital component is essential for the future of effective contemporary classroom experiences for both students and faculty.

Acknowledgements

We would like to acknowledge the contributions of several other NJIT colleagues in furthering the NJIT Converged Learning model and its successful implementation from its early stages through now. We thank Dr. Basil Baltzis for his efforts in ensuring the quality of pedagogy and technology support as well as coordinated course scheduling for socially distanced learning during the pandemic. The rapid expansion of converged learning demanded the efforts of Blake Haggerty and his team to equip classrooms with the necessary technologies and provide instructor support as well as the efforts of Andrew Christ and his group to fast-track alterations to the campus physical infrastructure allowing safe and continual access to instructional facilities for students and instructors. At the inception of converged learning in 2013, Dr. Charles Brooks volunteered to pilot and teach the initial offerings in this modality, paving the way for additional enhancements and expansion of the modality. Finally, we thank Dr. Eugene P. Deess and Dr. Yi Meng for their support in obtaining the data for this case study.

References

Deek, F. P., Deek, M. A., & Friedman, R. S. (1999). The virtual classroom experience: Viewpoints from computing and humanities. *Interactive Learning Environments, 7*(2-3), 113-136.

Hiltz, S. R. (1986). The "virtual classroom": Using computer-mediated communication for university teaching. *Journal of Communication, 36*(2), 95-104.

Office of the Provost, "2020 Vision: A Strategic Plan for NJIT" (2015).

Office of the Provost, "Convergence: A Vision and Framework for Leadership in Digital Learning" (2013).

Office of the Provost, "Pandemic Recovery Plan" (2020).

Opportunity Insights, "Social Capital Atlas" (2022).

United Nations Educational, Scientific and Cultural Organization, "Education in a post-COVID world: Nine ideas for public action" (2020).

U.S. Department of Education, "Education in a Pandemic: The Disparate Impacts of COVID-19 on America's Students" (2021).

Author Biographies

Fadi P Deek and Regina Collinsi

 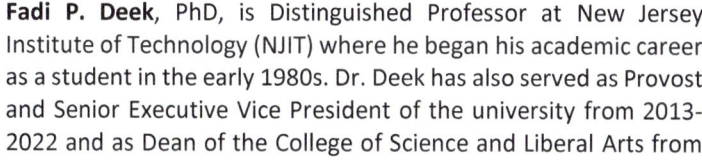

Fadi P. Deek, PhD, is Distinguished Professor at New Jersey Institute of Technology (NJIT) where he began his academic career as a student in the early 1980s. Dr. Deek has also served as Provost and Senior Executive Vice President of the university from 2013-2022 and as Dean of the College of Science and Liberal Arts from 2003-2013.

 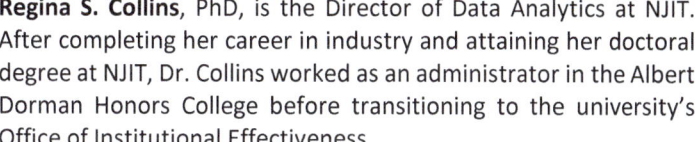

Regina S. Collins, PhD, is the Director of Data Analytics at NJIT. After completing her career in industry and attaining her doctoral degree at NJIT, Dr. Collins worked as an administrator in the Albert Dorman Honors College before transitioning to the university's Office of Institutional Effectiveness

Capsule: Supporting UK Undergraduate Medical Education

Nadia Mahmood[1], Chee Yeen Fung[2] Tim Vincent[1], Juliet Wright[1], Amir H. Sam[2], Malcolm Reed[1], Dawn Hanna[1], Peter Dennis[1], David C. Howlett[1],
[1]Brighton and Sussex medical school
[2]Imperial College London medical school
nadia.mahmood4@nhs.net
c.fung@imperial.ac.uk
t.r.vincent@bsms.ac.uk
juliet.wright6@nhs.net
a.sam@imperial.ac.uk
m.reed@bsms.ac.uk
d.hanna@bsms.ac.uk
p.b.dennis@bsms.ac.uk
david.howlett@nhs.net

Introduction and objectives

A key part of undergraduate medical training is clinical placements where students can actively apply a large volume of knowledge to a range of healthcare practices. The challenge for medical students and course leaders is both the volume of knowledge required and opportunity to apply this to all clinical situations as required by the Outcomes for Graduates curriculum of the General Medical Council (GMC; GMC 2018). This is particularly pertinent for the latter years of the course where students spend increasing time on clinical placements.

The Course team at Brighton and Sussex Medical School (BSMS) developed a bank of clinical case scenarios to capitalise on the pedagogical benefits of case-based learning in health professions education (Thistlethwaite et al 2012). Having initially provided the cases through the university of Brighton's Blackboard Learn® platform, student feedback indicated the primary importance of a high-quality digital experience. BSMS partnered with Ocasta, to deliver clinical case scenarios through a high-quality bespoke mobile and web interface. It was named 'Capsule' – Clinical and Professional Studies Unique Learning Environment – and launched in October 2016 to undergraduate medical students on clinical placement.

Capsule has been specifically designed to support medical students as adult learners (David 2013). The bank of clinical cases is free at the point of use for all medical students to access at any time during their course. This allows for readily available, self-directed learning to take place at any point during the undergraduate medical programme, regardless of the individual's curriculum structure. Each student is able to flexibly select cases to study in alignment with their clinical placements and either build on their existing knowledge and experience or prepare themselves for their next placement. The clinical orientation of each case, followed by the progressive question and answer format, further allows medical students to progress through a patient's journey. This methodology allows students to realistically solve problems as new patient information arises, which also assists in their role development as future doctors.

Substantial consideration had also been given to ensure the Capsule clinical cases readily guide the student user through Bloom's Taxonomy (1956). Cases open with a clinical vignette, which can be followed by questions testing basic clinical recall and understanding. As the patient journey progresses through the case, more information is made available to the student, such as further history, examination findings or investigation results. This allows students to apply existing knowledge, analyse the information given and evaluate the scenario which enables higher-order learning in tasks such as forming differential diagnoses and determining management plans.

Once a case is completed, scores and feedback for each individual question within the case is immediately given to the student, providing each user with a personalised learning resource. The breakdown of the feedback can particularly highlight areas which need further attention, bringing to the open pane of Johari's Window topics which may previously have been unknown or were blind spots for the student (Luft and Ingham 1955). Students are also able compare their scores with the group average which allows for important benchmarking and insight into their personal performance. Universities also have the option for providing tutors and faculty members access to student scores. This enables progress and performance tracking which can be useful in identifying students-in-difficulty.

The overall objectives of the Capsule learning resource are:

To provide students with a consistent opportunity to encounter the full range of clinical presentations and conditions of the curriculum and medical specialties. For students on geographically dispersed clinical placements, not all clinical presentations in the curriculum may be encountered or taught consistently. Capsule provides an applied learning resource that can provide students with a baseline exposure to all the applied knowledge for the course.

To provide a self-directed learning resource with content that is explicitly aligned to the curriculum, pitched at the correct level and validated by experienced clinical faculty. Research by course leads into popular commercial revision-focussed quiz banks revealed an inappropriate degree of inaccuracy or difficulty for medical students. All Capsule content is written by senior academic faculty and cases are routinely reviewed for accuracy and to ensure they are in line with up-to-date guidance.

To make the learning resource applicable to all medical students in the UK through alignment with the content with the Medical Licensing Assessment (MLA). This new national Assessment has been introduced by the GMC as a mandatory requirement for all Final Year medical students from the academic year 2024/25 for progression to postgraduate foundation training (GMC 2021). By aligning Capsule to the clinical content of this national assessment, it makes Capsule a valid learning tool for all UK medical schools.

To provide a high-quality and robust digital experience for users. As a non-compulsory, self-directed learning resource, it is particularly important that the digital experience encourages and enhances engagement rather than hindering. BSMS chose to invest in the provision of high-quality digital resource that is comparable to commercial-level apps and user experience.

To utilise a range of digital tools to maximise engagement and effectiveness. Capsule contains an extensive library of clinical case scenarios with questions in different formats (multiple choice, matching, and ordering). The content makes use of multimedia (e.g ECGs, X-rays, pathology specimens, clinical photos and videos) that support clinical interpretation skills required for medical practice. The platform includes features such as separate dedicated web and mobile app interfaces, topic searching, performance tracking, and a teaching mode for use in synchronous sessions.

To make Capsule free at the point of use for medical students. Research with students indicated the amount of personal funding spent on digital resources to support learning. We believe that all students should have access to a high-quality digital resource regardless of personal finances. Capsule is provided free of charge to students through direct funding from the school (not commercial sponsorship or advertising). Medical school partners have also decided to offer it free-of-charge to students.

The specific objective of the focus of this case study is:

To support undergraduate medical students during the Covid lockdown by providing Capsule to all UK medical schools for free. When the Covid lockdown in

March 2020 interrupted all clinical placements, Capsule was uniquely placed to provide students with an applied self-directed learning resource. Through sponsorship of the Medical Schools Council (MSC) and editorial input from Imperial College London, BSMS were able to make Capsule available to all UK medical schools free-of-charge for 18 months.

The infrastructure of Capsule

One of the unique aspects of Capsule is the unprecedented **quality and quantity of the educational content** created by a medical school specifically for undergraduate clinical students in one resource. Capsule contains over 720 clinical case scenarios comprising over 3500 questions, each with detailed feedback to maximise learning, and over 500 multimedia resources (e.g. photos and videos) to support clinical interpretation skills. This vast quantity of content has been written by senior clinical faculty and academic colleagues connected to BSMS. The content is reviewed by an editorial group and specialty leads to ensure curriculum alignment, medical accuracy, and consistency of presentation.[1]

Another key aspect of the learning resource is the **quality of the platform and the excellent user experience** it delivers. Extensive user research and feedback was conducted in the design phase to fully explore the user requirement. BSMS decided to partner with Ocasta, an experienced local digital solutions company, and invest in a bespoke high-quality, commercial-grade platform that would deliver all the functional requirements, and provide a robust digital experience for students and faculty. The mobile app is available on iOS and Android via the respective app stores which facilitates access and distribution to users globally.

The platform is feature-rich including:

- The full case library listed by colour-coded specialty group.
- Quiz-building tool for students to create bespoke collections of cases to suit specific learning goals and to share these between peers.
- Performance indicators including score breakdowns, strongest and weakest topics, and comparison with cohort averages
- Teaching-support functions including Presenter Mode for use in synchronous learning sessions and recommended Quizzes to direct students to certain topics/collections.

---

[1] When Capsule was rolled out to all UK medical schools during the lockdown, clinical faculty from other UK medical schools contributed to content editing, particularly those at Imperial College, London, for which we are grateful.

The platform is available to all users at https://learn.capsule.ac.uk. Further information is available at https://info.capsule.ac.uk and see the appendix below for example screenshots (Fig 1-6).

In Spring 2020, Ocasta undertook a platform development of Capsule to make sure it is compliant with digital accessibility requirements.

As well as the front-end interface, Capsule has a **bespoke back-end Case Management System (CMS)** that allows management of the case content and users, and also provides detailed data reporting for learning analytics and monitoring. It is built on a WordPress-based interface to make it user-friendly for non-technical authors and administrators.

Capsule also has a **built-in feedback feature** that allows users to query any content in a case (e.g. clinical enquiry or potential error). This dedicated feedback channel is managed by a team of three people in BSMS who respond and resolve queries in a timely fashion. It is a helpful additional mechanism for maintaining accuracy and inclusion of the student voice. Regular user surveys are also conducted via the platform.

The challenges and overcoming them
1. *Scaling up Capsule in 2020 to fulfil a UK-wide need for a digital learning resource for clinical medical students*

The Covid lockdown in March 2020 required medical schools to suspend all face-to-face teaching and clinical placements. There was concern that this would negatively impact knowledge acquisition and clinical competencies, especially in those students at the critical stage about to transition to postgraduate training. As a result, there was a critical and urgent need for alternative teaching methods that were digitally accessible but still able to provide highly-applied learning affordances. Capsule was uniquely placed to support this and was identified by the MSC as one of three digital learning resources that could help support UK medical students.

In April 2021, the MSC sponsored the necessary work to expand Capsule's capability to be offered free of charge to all 33 medical schools in the UK. BSMS and Ocasta partnered with Imperial College London to undertake a detailed content check, and Ocasta developed platform enhancements. Capsule was made free at the point of use for all UK medical students from the 1st of May 2020. BSMS, Imperial and Ocasta agreed to waive all costs and only cover baseline outlay to support Capsule. All UK medical schools registered with Capsule, a total of 41,404 medical students and 3,187 faculty.

2. Case Study: Use of Capsule at Imperial College School of Medicine

During the Covid-19 pandemic, Imperial College School of Medicine formally embedded Capsule into the undergraduate medical curriculum as a 'digital clinical placement' for the Years 3 and 5 students. Capsule cases were combined into weekly packages which simulated cases students would have seen on an equivalent face-to-face ward during their clinical placement. Teaching was delivered remotely in small groups in the form of a digital ward round using each Capsule case as a virtual patient.

As cases were pre-allocated for each teaching sessions, students were able to submit any questions regarding the cases ahead of the session and educators could prospectively plan and prepare their teaching material. The cases then formed the basis for discussion and teaching during the digital ward round in a similar fashion to that of a traditional ward round. As a result, Capsule was able to facilitate a much more tailored and focussed learning experience for the students.

Capsule also provided rich analytics of each individual student's interaction with the platform, giving timely, personalised performance feedback to both the student and their tutor. The data enabled longitudinal programmatic formative assessment showing progress throughout the course. This information was subsequently used to inform discussion in tutor-student academic meetings to highlight any areas of difficulty.

3. Tagging and alignment to the UK Medical Licensing Assessment content map

In order to maximise the effectiveness of Capsule as a learning resource, a team of clinical educators were recruited to map and tag the cases to the UK Medical Licensing Assessment (MLA) content map. This process enabled evaluation of Capsule coverage of the MLA content map and identification of areas for further development. Additionally, the tagging of Capsule cases enabled a substantially more effective search function, as cases could be found through keyword (tag) searches, which further improved the student user experience.

4. Global content quality assurance in April 2020 prior to UK school roll-out

To ensure all content was up to date and quality assured prior to the UK-wide rollout of Capsule, a large team of volunteer clinical editors from across UK medical schools worked with the Capsule team at BSMS to accomplish a full quality assurance review of all case content. This was to ensure all content was up to date, in line with current guidance, accurate, relevant, and pitched at the right level. This was made possible by extensive teamwork, collaboration, and recruitment of suitable volunteer editors.

5. Editorial and user support for queries from 40k students

In the last few years, Capsule has received over 800 student queries from both students and faculty across UK medical schools via the direct feedback function on the platform. Queries range from pointing out small typing/grammatical errors, to technical issues, to students wanting more detailed explanation as to why one option is correct over another. All queries are investigated, and any content edits made. In most cases, a direct response is provided to the student offering a detailed explanation. This personalised and meaningful feedback service is valuable for learning and for helping maintain content accuracy. The BSMS team has had to expand to meet this increased demand.

6. Platform development

Opening up Capsule to a much larger user-base, including international schools, required significant platform developments. Following the large-scale expansion, Ocasta increased user accounts from 4,000 to almost 50,000 to accommodate both students and faculty. Structural changes were required to manage multiple school tenancies using a single content dataset but allowing local access to local user groups with robust data management. A new 'bundling' and 'subscription' architecture was developed to allow for content release to be controlled and targeted for specific audiences. This functionality greatly increased the functional capability of Capsule and opened up its potential use for other user groups (e.g. other healthcare courses). As well as the MSC sponsorship, this development work was supported by a successful bid for a UK government Covid-19 related emergency grant.

7. Alignment with the Medical Licensing Assessment (MLA)

The original case content created for Capsule at its inception was in line with the undergraduate medical school curriculum at BSMS. However, since then the MLA has been introduced by the GMC, set to be mandatory requirement in 2024/25. To be an effective and relevant learning resource for UK students, Capsule content has to reflect the MLA curriculum, as well as local school curricular. Our own early investigations indicated that most commercial revision question banks lack this core alignment in a way that is validated by a UK medical school.

Comprehensive alignment of Capsule with the entire MLA Content Map was a significant challenge. While a large majority of the Capsule content was already covered, it required a thorough assessment of the present mapping to identify any gaps followed by 'tagging' of all 720 cases with relevant MLA content map 'tags' (metadata on all cases to enhance searching and mapping functionality).

This required a large volume of detailed work to be completed in a short timeframe. BSMS worked with Imperial College London and volunteer clinical faculty from other medical schools throughout April 2020 to map the existing case content to the MLA Content Map. A second process was then undertaken to edit existing cases and write additional ones to work towards 100% coverage of the MLA Content Map. This alignment work is almost complete with just a handful of cases being written by BSMS faculty in time for September 2022.

Reception and impact

Capsule has overwhelmingly met its original goals to support BSMS medical students with a comprehensive and applied learning resource in a high-quality platform, free at the point of need. Formal and informal feedback from students and faculty has remained overwhelmingly positive. Capsule has been consistently highly rated in annual student feedback processes, citing its accuracy, scope, and digital functionality as well as it being free of charge. Some example quotes from student feedback are included in the appendix, Fig 7.

Uptake and utilisation of Capsule following the national sponsorship by the MSC has been extensive. Currently up to 24000 cases are being completed per week (Fig. 8) and there are over 3000 active users most months (Fig 9). The intensive efforts by volunteer clinical faculty to prepare the content and the work by Ocasta to enhance the platform, enabled students to continue to access a highly-applied learning resource throughout lockdown. In addition, Capsule enabled educators to use the case-based learning format to be embedded into existing learning resources and into synchronous seminars and revision sessions as an additional teaching tool.

In light of the national roll-out, BSMS initiated a Capsule Educator Forum (CEF) – an open forum for representatives from all UK medical schools using Capsule. Online meetings provide opportunity for to communicate new developments within Capsule, receive an update on recent/upcoming technical developments from Ocasta, and for medical school partners to discuss their use of Capsule and offer comments, feedback, and suggestions for improvement.

When sponsorship by the MSC ended in August 2021, Capsule remained available as a fully managed software-as-a-service resource, run as a not-for profit service, for UK medical schools and those across the world. To date, there are 26 UK schools subscribing to Capsule and an increase in the number of international partners. Annual fees for the service are directed to supporting technical demands via Ocasta and BSMS staff resource for maintaining the support service.

Learning Outcomes

The unique nature of Capsule makes it ideal for education research. A study conducted at BSMS by Sadler *et al* in 2019 on a Final Year cohort of students, found that students who completed more Capsule cases tended to score higher per case. Overall, completing cases did give a small percentage increase in decile performance. This study suggests that Capsule is an effective learning resource with possible direct correlation with exam performance.

Future development

1. International expansion

The clinical case-based structure of Capsule and its universal digital platform means it has great potential for use in other medical and healthcare courses. It has already gained interest internationally and is being used in several medical schools:

Australia: One of our international partners is the University of Tasmania in Australia. We have been closely collaborating with medical education fellows there to create a single set of cases that cover both the Australian and UK undergraduate medical curricular. As part of this process, the medical education team at the University of Tasmania have re-reviewed every case and suggested changes as appropriate, adding another layer of quality control. Ocasta have created separate bundles for UK and Australia students to accommodate the differences in local practice and embedded these into the platform.

Rwanda: There are ongoing efforts to partner with medical schools in Sub-Saharan Africa to offer relevant Capsule content free to students and to support the delivery of undergraduate medical education in regions where students may struggle to access learning content. In collaboration with the medical education team in Rwanda, bespoke cases have been created to tailor to that curriculum and ensure coverage of the diseases that are more prevalent in Sub-Saharan Africa, for example tropical diseases. These specialist cases are also available to other students enrolled in other countries. In addition, a team of Capsule support staff are planned to travel to Rwanda to run workshops with local medical educators to generate more cases in line with the local curriculum.

Ukraine: Considering the recent events in Ukraine and subsequent disruption to medical student training, Capsule has been offered free at the point of use to medical schools in Ukraine. Further information here: https://www.capsule.ac.uk/blog/welcoming-ukrainian-medical-schools-and-their-students-to-capsule

2. Platform enhancement

BSMS and Ocasta continue to develop the platform itself to ensure it is responsive to the needs of learners and educators in a rapidly evolving digital landscape. Continual feedback is obtained from students via the reporting feedback tool and user surveys. It is consistently positive in regard to both content and platform and no major platform functions have been requested – testament to its meeting the learner need. Feedback is also sought from senior faculty at medical schools via a Capsule Educator Forum (to ascertain if there are any features that need changing or introducing to meet user needs. Examples of upcoming platform developments include enhancing the usage data reporting tools for local administrators and delivering capability for single sign-on (SSO) authentication.

References

Bloom, Benjamin S. Taxonomy of Educational Objectives: The Classification of Educational Goals. New York: Longmans, Green, 1956. Print.

David C. M. Taylor & Hossam Hamdy (2013) Adult learning theories: Implications for learning and teaching in medical education: AMEE Guide No. 83, Medical Teacher, 35:11, e1561-e1572, DOI: 10.3109/0142159X.2013.828153

GMC 2018 https://www.gmc-uk.org/education/standards-guidance-and-curricula/standards-and-outcomes/outcomes-for-graduates, accessed 4/7/22

GMC 2021 https://www.gmc-uk.org/education/medical-licensing-assessment/uk-medical-schools-guide-to-the-mla/mla-content-map, accessed 4/7/22

Karunaratne D, Karunaratne N, Wilmot J, Vincent T, Wright J, Mahmood N, Tang A, Sam AH, Reed M, Howlett D. *An Online Teaching Resource to Support UK Medical Student Education During the COVIDCovid-19 Pandemic: A Descriptive Account*. Adv Med Educ Pract. 2021 Nov 13;12:1317-1327. doi: 10.2147/AMEP.S337544. PMID: 34803422; PMCID: PMC8599888.

Luft, J. and Ingham, H. (1955) 'The Johari window, a graphic model of interpersonal awareness', Proceedings of the western training laboratory in group development. Los Angeles: UCLA.

Sadler J, Wright J, Vincent T, Kurka T, Howlett D. 2020. *What is the impact of Apps in medical education? A study of CAPSULECapsule, a case-based learning App*. BMJ Simulation and Technology Enhanced Learning [Internet].:bmjstel–2020. http://dx.doi.org/10.1136/bmjstel-2020-000593.

Thistlethwaite JE *et al*. 2012. The effectiveness of case- based learning in health professional education. A BEME systematic review: BEME Guide No. 23, Medical Teacher, 34:6, e421-e444, DOI: 10.3109/0142159X.2012.680939 Appendix

Figure 1: Capsule homepage. This dashboard provides a snapshot into how many cases the student has completed and scores.

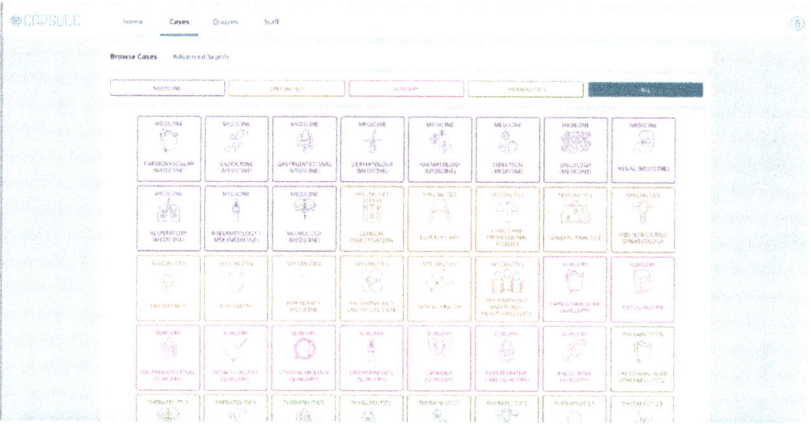

Figure 2: Clicking on the cases tab brings up an overview of the specialities, allowing student to complete cases by speciality.

Figure 3: The quizzes tab allow student to create their quizzes or view shared quizzes.

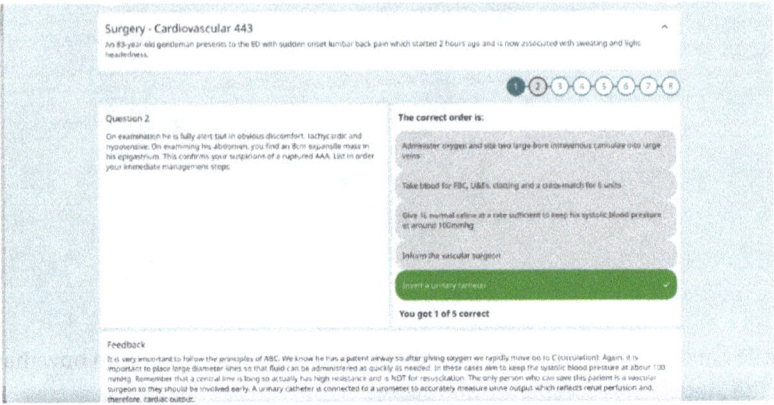

Figure 4: Example of a multiple-choice question, with feedback.

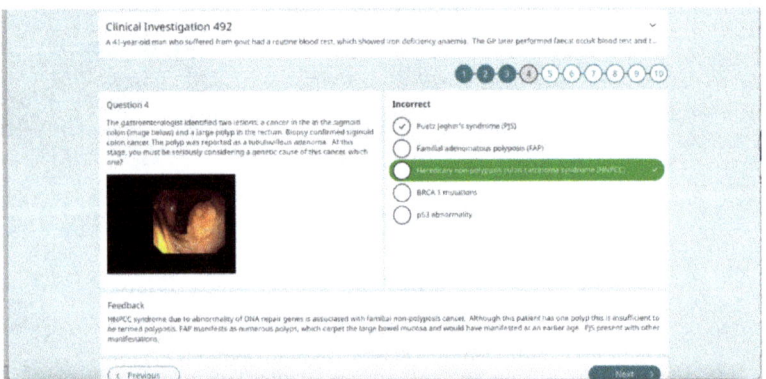

Figure 5: Example of a ranking question from Capsule.

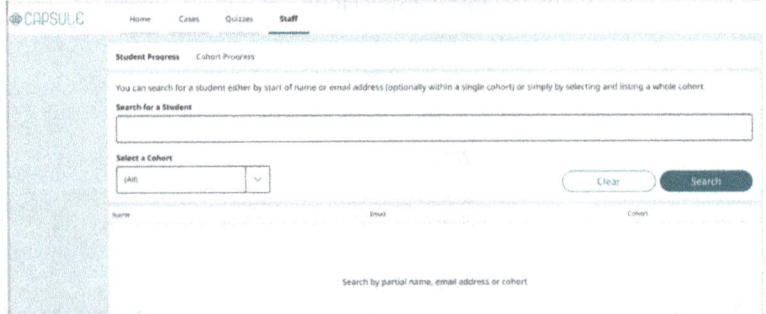

Figure 6: Staff tab allows faculty to view individual student progress.

> "Really good cases with thoughtful questions and excellent feedback/explanation on answers."

> The fact that we get to study with cases and follow through from diagnosis to treatment. It helps me consider aspects of management I would not have previously. The questions are at an appropriate level.

> The application of knowledge to work through a case is realistic to questions doctors ask on placement. I use it after I've made revision notes to check my understanding and apply knowledge to cases/ exam questions

> I like the case based questioning - and how the story unfolds within the case. The feedback is also really valuable

> i enjoy the range of questions and the depth of the questions. good for revising what you do and do not know about conditions. i like how can choose specialties.

> "I love that the cases and questions are written in the same structure as I would have it in an exam. The rationales given for the answers are very helpful as they further help me build my knowledge. This has been a wonderful study resource for me."

Figure 7: Student feedback received.

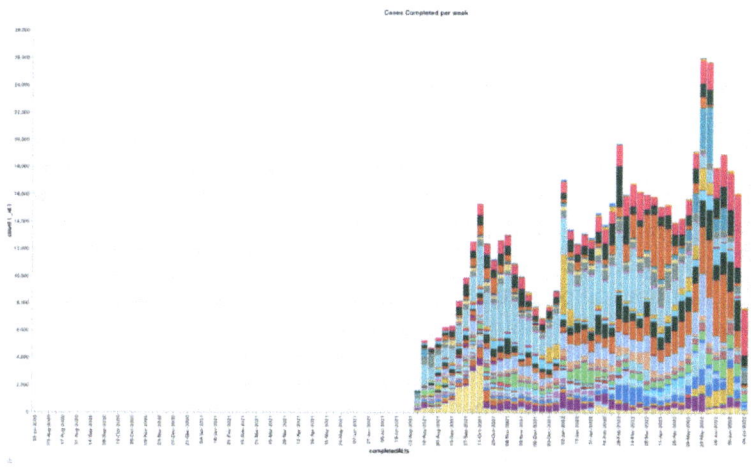

Figure 8: Number of capsule cases completed per week.

Eighth International e-Learning Excellence Awards

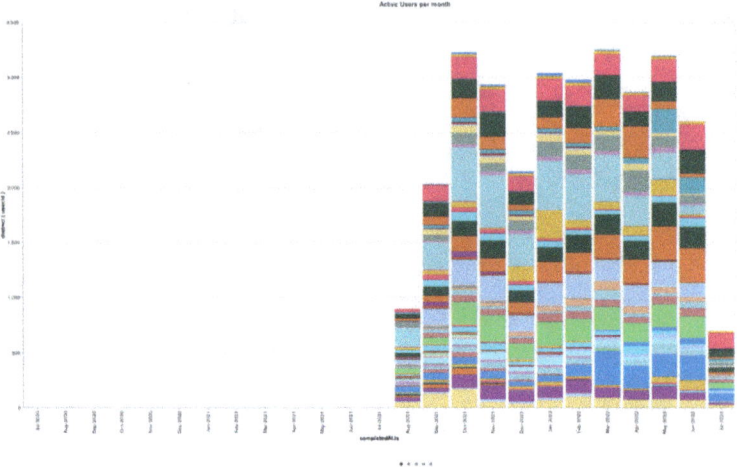

Figure 9: Number of active Capsule users per month.

Author Biographies

Nadia Mahmood studied medicine at King's College University of London and graduated in 2015 to undertake her foundation training at Guy's and St Thomas' Hospital in London. She completed an intercalated BSc in infectious diseases and immunobiology in and graduated with first class honours degree, also receiving a national prize from the British Society of immunology. She was awarded research funding by the St Thomas's Wegner's trust to continue important research in Granulomatosis with Polyangiitis patients.

Dr Chee Yeen Fung is the Preparedness for Practice Development Lead at Imperial College School of Medicine. Dr Fung also holds national educational and leadership roles at Health Education England, the Medical School Council and the General Medical Council, working on a range of educational leadership, assessment and widening participation projects.

Juliet Wright is a graduate from Guy's and St Thomas's Hospitals Professor Juliet Wright trained in general and geriatric medicine in the South West Thames region. She was awarded her MD from the University of Surrey for a study investigating recombinant human growth hormone in older patients undergoing elective knee replacement surgery.

 **David Howlett** is a Consultant Radiologist based at Eastbourne Hospital and is honorary Clinical Professor at Brighton and Sussex Medical School. He is Capsule academic lead and has been involved with the project since its inception in 2018. Prof Howlett is research active with approaching 600 publications and presentations and has written/edited numerous textbooks and book chapters.

open.uom.lk: A free online knowledge sharing platform

Vishaka Nanayakkara, Buddhika Karunarathne, Malik Ranasinghe, Amal Shehan Perera, Gayashan Amarasinghe, Sandareka Wickramanayake, Supunmali Ahangama, Kulani Mahadewa, Chathuranga Hettiarachchi
University of Moratuwa, Katubedda, Sri Lanka
Hasith Yaggahavita, 99x Technology, Colombo, Sri Lanka
vishaka@cse.mrt.ac.lk, buddhika@cse.mrt.ac.lk, malik@uom.lk, shehan@cse.mrt.ac.lk, gayashan@cse.mrt.ac.lk, sandarekaw@cse.mrt.ac.lk, supunmali@uom.lk, kulanim@uom.lk, chathuranga@cse.mrt.ac.lk, hasithy@99x.io

Abstract: 94% of the manpower requirement for the IT industry in Sri Lanka is for software developers. This demand cannot be met by IT graduates produced by all the higher education institutions in Sri Lanka. An industry ready trainee software developer needs to have the relevant skills but not necessarily a degree in IT. A student aspiring to enter a university in Sri Lanka has to wait nearly 5 months after finishing their Advanced level (university entrance) exams to receive their results and then another 8 months to start university. A student who is selected to enter university will be idle for nearly a year, and those who are unable to enter will be idle for 5 months until they receive their results and before they can consider their next step. To solve both problems, the University of Moratuwa developed the Trainee Full Stack Developer (TFSD) as a CSR initiative. TFSD is a six-month, six module online programme, offered free of charge to teach students the knowledge, skills and attitudes necessary to enter the IT industry as a trainee software developer. The online programme was developed in collaboration with IT industry professionals, and trains students with no prior knowledge in IT to be industry ready at the end of the course. The program consists of two modules in Python, three modules in Web Development and a final module consisting of Professional Practices and a Capstone project. All the formative and summative assessments and the capstone project are auto-graded to handle large volumes of assessments and provide instant feedback. The program, which is self-paced, targets students who have sat for their Advanced level exams and are awaiting results. The TFSD program which was launched on 22 February 2022 to coincide with completion of the Advanced level exams in 2022 has enrolled over 100,000 students as of 6th July 2022. Nearly 25% of the student cohort who sat for the exam in 2022 enrolled within 100 days of the course launch.

Introduction

The world of education is fast adapting to online learning methods. The concepts of online learning, e-learning and distance learning have been the focus for many studies on pedagogical delivery and effectiveness (Johnson, Hornik and Salas, 2008; Mahdizadeh, Biemans and Mulder, 2008; Moore, Dickson-Deane and Galyen, 2011; Parkes, Stein and Reading, 2015).

In Sri Lanka only around 30% of those who qualify for higher education from GCE Advanced (A) Level Examinations secure placements in either public or private sector Higher Education Institutions. The time between completing the A Level Exams and the release of results is about five months and university selection is nearly a year.

A key policy area of Vistas of Prosperity and Splendour (National Policy Framework Vistas of Prosperity and Splendour 2019), the National Policy Framework of the Government of Sri Lanka (GOSL), is to promote a Technology Based Society in Sri Lanka, by developing a Global Innovation Hub and promoting IT Entrepreneurship. The Sri Lankan Computing (IT) industry

The infrastructure

The Trainee Full Stack Developer course is hosted on the Open Learning Platform, which utilises the Moodle learning management system (https://moodle.org/). Moodle is an open-source learning management system which was developed using pedagogical principles. It is also the platform that is being used at the University of Moratuwa as the eLearning platform. Moodle provides a variety of plugins, which is software that adds new functions, enabling the inclusion of additional interactive teaching and learning activities and to make the management of the course easier. These plugins can be categorised into activities and resources. Activities generally enable interactions with students, among students, and/or with the teacher. This includes forums, assignments, and quizzes etc. Resources allow the teacher to provide access to content such as a file, folder, page, book, or a URL to an external website. The Open Learning Platform utilises the full spectrum of the Moodle plugins.

The Moodle - plugins such as quiz activities, file, page, and book resources, H5P tool (further discussed in Section 2.1), along with the CodeRunner activity, and the embedded Trinket tool have formed the complete Open Learning Platform which is now being used actively by thousands of students. Further, the completion of TFSD is marked by a capstone project which is conducted in fully automated manner using GitHub classroom (Section 2.2) allows the Open Learning Platform to handle large volumes of project submissions without burdening the instructors.

One of the main objectives of the Open Learning Platform is to provide a self-learning portal to the students. We identified the need to automatically grade the programme code the students develop as part of their learning activities. CodeRunner (Lobb and Harlow, 2016; Croft and England, 2020) is an automated programming assessment plugin for Moodle, that is also used in internal courses at the Faculty of Engineering at University of Moratuwa. CodeRunner provides the ability to automatically grade programming assignments and allows the teachers to set the assignment as a Moodle quiz (Figure 1).

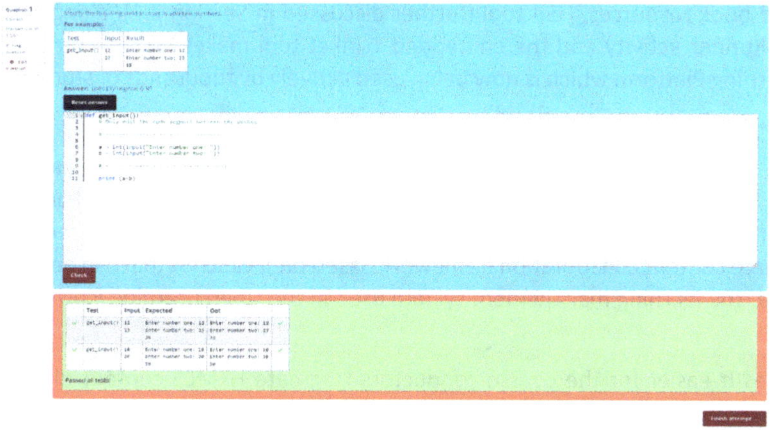

Figure 1. An example CodeRunner quiz activity that illustrates a programming assignment given to students, the answers provided by the student, and the results generated by evaluating the test cases.

The teacher can set the language of the programming assignment, the conditions for passing the assignment and the test cases needed to evaluate the assignment, among other options. Once a student submits their answer to a question as a programme code, it is executed in an isolated environment in a sandbox server (referred as the JOBE server) and evaluated against the test cases set by the teacher. Depending on the grading criteria, the student receives a mark for their submission as soon as this evaluation is completed, which generally occurs within a few seconds. Therefore, the student receives immediate feedback for the activity allowing the student to learn constructively. The user evidence that we have collected (Section 4) has elevated the end user experience of CodeRunner by the students as intuitive and rewarding.

Providing hands-on programming experience is another main objective of the courses provided at the Open Learning Platform. As a result, we identified the need to allow the students to code on the platform itself (on a web browser) without installing any additional software or programming environments. We have used Trinket (Kurniawati, Kusumaningsih and Sophan, 2018) which is a web-based tool that allows the user to write python code, execute code, and generate outputs, inside the browser (Figure 2). We use trinket to provide the coding playground that allows users to code, engage in self-evaluation and build on their knowledge by themselves. Trinket is added to the Moodle course as an embedded web resource.

The Moodle learning management system, the plugins such as quiz activities, file, page, and book resources, H5P tool (further discussed in Section 2.1), along with the CodeRunner activity and the embedded Trinket tool makes up the complete Open Learning Platform which is now being used actively by thousands of students.

1.1 Content Arrangement with H5P

Providing interactive content to the users is crucial in a self-paced learning platform. In the Open Learning Platform – UOM, we use the H5P - HTML5 Package (H5P) framework to offer interactive content to the students. H5P is a free and open-source content collaboration framework based on JavaScript that can be used in Moodle, the learning management system used in the Open Learning Platform – UOM.

H5P makes it easier for the course conductors to create HTML5 content directly from the browser window. Further, H5P is mobile-friendly, allowing the users of our platform to enjoy the same interactive learning experience using smartphones and tablets.

H5P enables the creation of interactive content like interactive videos, presentations, games, and many more. We extensively use interactive videos on our platform. Using interactive videos in H5P allows us to add many different types of questions and informational resources to the lecture videos. For example, we can add multiple choice, fill-in-the-blank questions, pop-up text, and interactive summaries (Figure 3).

In addition to making the videos more engaging, we can encourage the students to learn the lessons thoroughly using the interactions and features offered by H5P. For instance, we can add interactive questions with adaptive behaviour in the middle of the lecture video. Typically, the lecture video is paused for the question, and the correct answer allows the student to proceed with the video. However, if the wrong answer is given, we can configure it to direct the user to the place where the answer to the question is presented. Furthermore, H5P allows disabling video fast forwarding to encourage the student to watch the complete video and prevents them from skipping watching the video.

At the end of the interactive video, the students are shown a summary of the interactive questions they answered, along with the marks they obtained for each question.

Figure 2. Trinket is embedded as a tool inside a lecture note to allow the student to try and execute a program code within the web browser and to observe outputs.

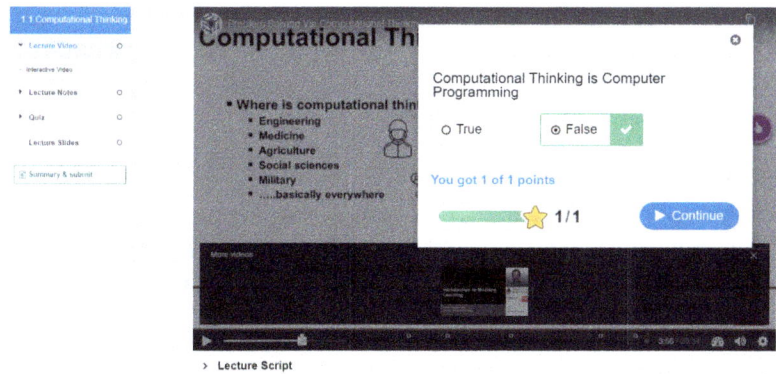

Figure 3. An example where the student is asked an interactive question during the lecture.

Hence, using H5P provides formative assessment opportunities for the students while making it enjoyable to watch the lecture video.

1.2 GitHub Classroom

As thoroughly evaluating the students' programming skills is essential when conducting IT courses, in the Open Learning Platform – UoM, students are given programming assignments at the end of each programming course. In addition, at the end of the TFSD Program, the students are given a capstone project to assess the knowledge students gained via the program.

We conduct this capstone project using GitHub Classroom (GitHub Classroom), which provides an exciting learning environment for the students by facilitating automatic grading and instant feedback. In an assignment created using GitHub

Classroom, we can provide a template repository with the initial code base for students to start the coding. Further, the GitHub Classroom facilitates auto-grading. We can configure automatic test cases to evaluate the code committed by the students. If all tests succeed for a commit, a green checkmark will be displayed for the students. If not, a red X will be displayed. Hence, the students can check their work as soon as they commit the code to an assignment repository. Furthermore, students can see the entire history of test runs.

They are also allowed to view the details of the evaluation, such as compilation errors and test case failures which provide the students with a great learning experience. GitHub Classroom also facilitates the course conductors to monitor the students' progress for the given assignment. For example, the course conductors can check how many of the enrolled students have accessed the assignment, the commit history of each student, how many points each student has gained, and which students are struggling. Hence, employing GitHub classrooms has enabled the Open Learning Platform to conduct coding projects in a more scalable and sustainable manner.

The Challenges

The courses were created in collaboration with the IT industry to ensure the learners will have the skills required to enter the industry and meet its needs. Collaborations with the industry have guaranteed that the programme will be fulfilling the objective of producing learners who will help fulfil the human capital requirements of the IT industry. TFSD is endorsed by the Computer Society of Sri Lanka (CSSL) and Sri Lanka Association for Software Services Companies (SLASSCOM) which are leading organisations which represent the IT industry in Sri Lanka. Endorsement by CSSL and the recognition from SLASSCOM are encouraging. The voluntary support from IT professionals and the financial support from DP Education foundation has enabled the University to provide this course free of charge to all learners without requiring any government funding.

With vastly growing participation numbers, one of the major challenges was the management of assessments. Adding any manual grading component was impractical at such a large scale. Therefore, all the assessments had to be designed with provisions for auto-grading and using a variety of question types supported by the Moodle platform. The programming assessments were prepared using the CodeRunner question type, which supports auto-grading and feedback.

It should be emphasised that the platform has successfully adopted auto-grading techniques, so that it minimises the requirement for any manual grading effort. The process of completing all six courses of the programme is automated, so that the certificate for each course is generated in real-time once all the assessment requirements are satisfied by the participant. The assessments are constantly being reviewed and necessary changes are made so that the authenticity of evaluations is preserved to the extent possible through the platform.

Due to the asynchronous nature of delivery of the courses, retaining the interest level of the participants was also a major challenge. Unlike in live delivery of lectures, the risk of reduced participant engagement was considerably high. This was addressed at the stage of video content development by using example use cases to relate to the lesson content. After the video production interactive content was added to the video lesson using the resources provided by the H5P content arrangement module.

We were also faced with the socio-cultural factor connected with the unfamiliarity of the method of delivery of the learning programme. The participants are mostly used to teacher-centred education rather than learner-centred education. This is rather a broader issue that must be addressed at different stages of the education system. We expect this learning program would be a step towards making a positive change. In this program we provide multiple communication channels to the participants, so that they are provided the assistance where necessary.

How the initiative received by the participants

The open.uom.lk platform has reached over 130,000 participants in all twenty-five districts in Sri Lanka within the short duration after the launch of the platform.

To understand the progression and completions, the progress of students in activities in individual courses are closely monitored. Figure 4 depicts the number of users who have completed individual activities of Course 1 - Python for Beginners. The progression from one section to the next is dependent on students completing the activities of the section with the required pass mark. As these assessments are formative, students were given five attempts to obtain the required mark. In most activities the completed and passed bars were indicating the same numbers. However, Section 4.2 and 4.3 the coding assignments have given rise to the difference in completed vs Passed. This necessitated a detailed look at how the students have participated in the example coding exercises in the previous sections. While the data is not available for interactions of all programming exercises using Trinket, wherever it was available it showed low interaction.

Eighth International e-Learning Excellence Awards

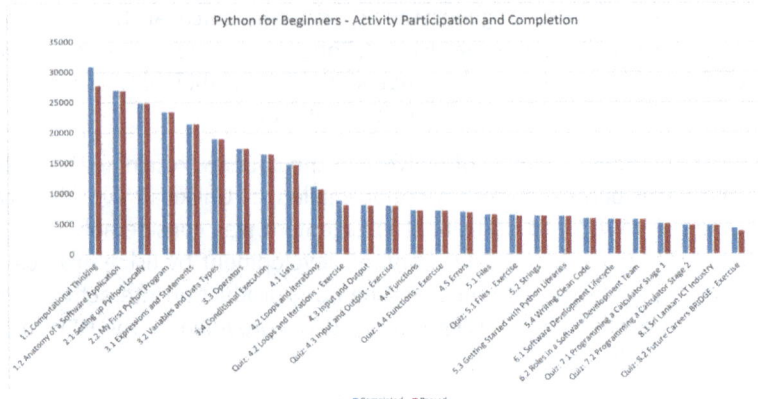

Figure 4. Course 1 - Python for Beginners - Activity Completion

As the students are making progress at their own pace, the shape of the graph was expected. However, the analysis of this nature enables the development team to identify the areas which can be further improved. Focused group discussions with students from selected categories were helpful in identifying how the instructions can be further improved. Need to reiterate the importance of following instruction including performing the coding using Trinket was identified as many students are not interacting with them.

Furthermore, three students who had successfully completed the six courses were interviewed. The open-ended questions based on the Delone-McLean information system success model (Delone and McLean, 2003) focused on three different aspects: (a) information quality (ease of understanding, briefness, use of relatable examples, relevance, and links between courses); (b) system quality (flexibility, reliability, consistency, and availability); and (c) service quality (responsiveness) of the Moodle-based courses. To understand the improvements in knowledge, skills, and attitudes, questions about satisfaction and net benefit from the courses were also asked. Table 1 contains the responses of the student respondents with respective consent.

The objective of the TFSD programme was to provide the knowledge, skills and attitudes required for a candidate to start as an intern in an IT company without being a burden to the organisation. The stringent order of completion was maintained to achieve this objective assuming no prior experience.

Table 1. Results of participant interviews

Information quality:
Response 1: "Angular content was really good. A beginner can easily learn. I initially didn't know Angular. I feel the content is valuable since it covers the basics well."
Response 2: "Could learn something extra than what I already knew."
Reponse 3: "It was the first time I learned Angular. I learned quite a few new things regarding Angular."
Response 4: "My brother who just joined the Engineering faculty of Moratuwa started following the Python course. He finds it useful as he had no prior programming knowledge or experience."
Response 5: "I have used MVC architecture in my project, but I didn't have a good understanding of the folder structure. I learned it through the Capstone project.."
System quality:
Response 1: "No issues regarding the system quality"
Service quality:
Response 1: "It would be better if captions were added to the lecture videos and allowed for changing video quality from lower to higher resolutions."
Response 2: "The interactive forum in Course 6C is very useful. It encourages communication among the students and also with the instructors to clarify the problems."
Satisfaction and Net benefit:
Response 1: "...useful for projects....."
Response 2: "I have never thought of using Angular, but now my knowledge is increased because of the course.... initially I used Laravel.. Now looking for training opportunities in Angular too."
Response 3: "......made more familiar with industry jargons, standards, problem solving strategies ...got the exposure to how things communicate in the industry"
Response 4: "Overall I'm very satisfied with the courses"
Response 5: "..will be useful when applying for an internship. I could add the new skills to my CV and share my certificates on LinkedIn."
Response 6: "I would like to recommend these courses to my friends."
Response 7: "The Capstone project has given me the confidence that I could do well in something new without prior knowledge."

However, discussions with users have revealed that there may be some experienced users who may want to not do the first two courses. Also, whether there is a usefulness in offering programmes with different combinations of the modules is some aspect worth investigating into.

The Learning Outcomes

The main objective is for the participant, on completing the course, to have the skills and knowledge required to enter the IT industry as an intern or at an entry level. The course aimed to provide a foundation so anyone, even if they lacked any previous experience or knowledge on programming will be able to complete the course via independent learning.

A dedicated team of analysts ensured the course was benchmarked against the best programmes currently available worldwide. Constant guidance from the experts in education ensured the quality and relevance of the course material. The experts from the IT industry helped shape the programme so that it produces industry-ready personnel upon successful completion.

The programme consists of six courses which aims to methodically build participants' knowledge and skills as a full stack developer.

- Python for Beginners (Introduction to programming)
- Web Design for Beginners (Introduction to web technologies)
- Python Programming (Foundation for advanced programming)
- Front-End Web Development (Single page application development)
- Server-Side Web Programming (Handling and serving data)
- Professional Practice in Software Development (Attitude development and capstone project)

The course content was designed to be delivered with recorded videos and supplementary reading materials. Each lesson consists of one or more recorded videos, lecture notes, lecture slides, interactive activities, and self-assessments. The script for each video lesson was included so that the participants can carefully follow the lesson and extract as much information as required by each individual and to make it more accessible to students who are not fluent in English so they can use translation applications if they find a word or section difficult to understand. The video lessons include embedded interactive content which helps to keep the participant engaged and prevents students from skipping the video. The lecture note provides additional information on the lesson, links to further reading resources, and may consist of built-in programming exercises using Trinket (Kurniawati, Kusumaningsih and Sophan, 2018) to help the participant to enhance their skills and internalise the content that is covered in the respective section.

Each section contains assessments to monitor and evaluate student progress of the courses. The assessments may include quizzes and programming exercises using auto graded CodeRunner (Lobb, R. and Harlow, J. 2016). The participants are required to attempt the quizzes and obtain a satisfactory grade to proceed to the next section. The assessments are similar to the assessments available on leading online learning platforms such as Coursera, Edx, Udemy, Udacity etc. However, there are no peer-graded assignments in our platform. Most of the assessments are auto graded, but there are few assignments which are manually graded by our instructors to ensure that the students completing the course have the required skill set. Unlike in other platforms we have a team from the Centre for Open and Distance Learning (CODL) to continuously monitor and give support for the learners to enhance their learning experience.

The main advantage of our platform is we are providing all the course content and certificates for free making it accessible to the local students who otherwise would not be able to afford similar courses. Similar existing platforms have free courses or financial aid programs with certain limitations. For example, a fee of 39$ per month in the Coursera platform is not bearable for most Sri Lankan students. We have designed our course content considering the local school syllabus to ensure the course is accessible for students from different education levels.

Plans to further develop the initiative

With all six modules launched and learners completing the course, the next phase is to provide them industry internships. Building on the industry awareness created through SLASSCOM and CSSL, a meeting with Sri Lankan IT Industry CXOs and their Human Resource counterpart will be organised. Industry will also be facilitated to interact with the learners who complete all six modules using the same platform and first 100 participants who successfully complete the programme will be awarded internship placements at partnering IT companies at a national level event to create more awareness and to increase the confidence on the programme.

We expect continuous improvement of the programme by taking the participant feedback into consideration. We constantly receive constructive feedback on where we can improve and provide additional support to broaden the audience.

We are in the process of developing local language support in our platform which is highly beneficial for the students with low English language proficiency. As the first step we have included translations in local (Sri Lankan) languages (Sinhalese and Tamil) for the lecture script in Course 1 - Python for beginners. Figure 5 shows how the translations are included in the lecture script view.

In the meantime, we constantly provide local language support only when aiding individuals when requested and for the initial basic instructions about the registration etc.

The Sri Lankan school system provides IT courses to students; however, lack of widespread teacher training programs is a major problem preventing IT from being taught at secondary school level. Working together with the National Institute of Education (NIE), the main body responsible for providing teacher training, we plan to use the TFSD course and open.uom.lk platform to train the ICT teachers of the country on core skills required.

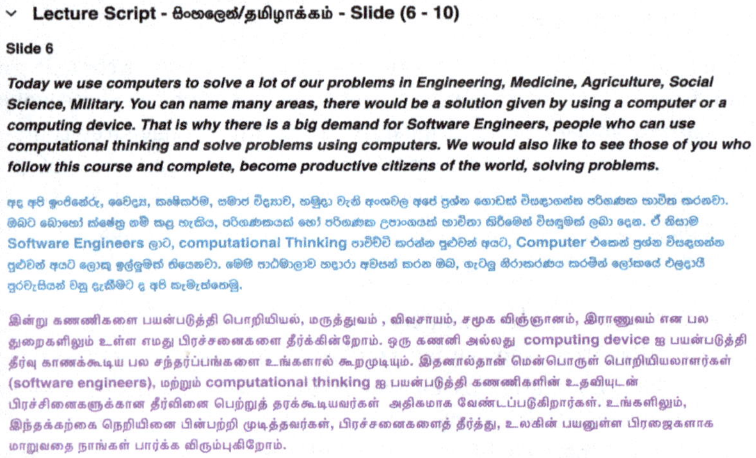

> **Lecture Script - සිංහලෙන්/தமிழாக்கம் - Slide (6 - 10)**
>
> Slide 6
>
> *Today we use computers to solve a lot of our problems in Engineering, Medicine, Agriculture, Social Science, Military. You can name many areas, there would be a solution given by using a computer or a computing device. That is why there is a big demand for Software Engineers, people who can use computational thinking and solve problems using computers. We would also like to see those of you who follow this course and complete, become productive citizens of the world, solving problems.*
>
> අද අපි ඉංජිනේරු, වෛද්‍ය, කෘෂිකර්ම, සමාජ විද්‍යාව, හමුදා වැනි අංශවල අපේ ප්‍රශ්න ගොඩක් විසඳාගන්න පරිගණක භාවිත කරනවා. ඔබට බොහෝ ක්ෂේත්‍ර තම් කළ හැකිය, පරිගණකයක් හෝ පරිගණක උපාංගයක් භාවිතා කිරීමෙන් විසඳුමක් ලබා දෙනු. ඒ නිසාම Software Engineers ලාට, computational Thinking භාවිට කරන්න පුළුවන් අයට, Computer එකෙන් ප්‍රශ්න විසඳගන්න පුළුවන් අයට ලොකු ඉල්ලුමක් තියෙනවා. මෙම පාඨමාලාව හදාරා අවසන් කරන ඔබ, දැඩිල කිරාසරක්ම කරන්නේ ලෝකයේ ඵලදායී පුරවැසියන් වනු ඇතිම්ම ද අපි බැලමැන්තමකි.

> இன்று கணணிகளை பயன்படுத்தி பொறியியல், மருத்துவம், விவசாயம், சமூக விஞ்ஞானம், இராணுவம் என பல துறைகளிலும் உள்ள எமது பிரச்சனைகளை தீர்க்கின்றோம். ஒரு கணனி அல்லது computing device ஐ பயன்படுத்தி தீர்வு காணக்கூடிய பல சந்தர்ப்பங்களை உங்களால் கூறமுடியும். இதனால்தான் மென்பொருள் பொறியியலாளர்கள் (software engineers), மற்றும் computational thinking ஐ பயன்படுத்தி கணணிகளின் உதவியுடன் பிரச்சினைகளுக்கான தீர்வினை பெற்றுத் தரக்கூடியவர்கள் அதிகமாக வேண்டப்படுகிறார்கள். உங்களிலும், இந்தக்கற்கை நெறியினை பின்பற்றி முடித்தவர்கள், பிரச்சனைகளைத் தீர்த்து, உலகின் பயனுள்ள பிரஜைகளாக மாறுவதை நாங்கள் பார்க்க விரும்புகிறோம்.

Figure 5. Original script in English followed by Sinhalese and Tamil translations

Leveraging on the acceptance of properly developed online programs to reach those who aspire to increase their knowledge, capabilities and capacity, especially during a time of economic hardships in Sri Lanka, open.uom.lk platform will soon launch online programs on Digital Entrepreneurship and Freelancing, and a conversion master's program on Project Management.

The objectives of the conversion master's program are to provide knowledge free of charge to any project participant interested in understanding the fundamentals of project management, and to convert qualified participants to enter the field of project management through the qualification.

A twelve (12) 3-credit module is being developed such that the Intended Learning Outcomes of the 12 modules will meet the Learning Objectives of the internationally recognised USA, Project Management Institute (PMI)'s new Exam Content Outline (ECO) commencing in October 2022, for its entry level qualification called the Certified Associate in Project Management (CAPM). The twelve 3-credit modules are launched independently allowing the participants the opportunity to obtain skills and knowledge on those areas or obtaining a conversion master's degree from the University of Moratuwa, Sri Lanka by stacking credits earned from completing the individual modules.

Industry has reached out with the requirements for more courses and arrangements are being made to offer new courses in the areas of Data Science, Software Quality Assurance, Cloud computing and Information Security. One major software company operating in Colombo has offered to develop content for a programming course in another language.

University and DP education foundation is working together with multiple communities to enhance the student completion rates of the programme. The unprecedented numbers registered, and the unique techniques incorporated to enhance knowledge, skills and attitudes of learners together with industry acceptance has given open.uom.lk the recognition of de facto platform for online learning in the country.

References

Delone, W. and McLean, E. (2003) The DeLone and McLean Model of Information Systems Success: A Ten-Year Update. J. of Management Information Systems. 19. 9-30. 10.1080/07421222.2003.11045748.

Croft, D. and England, M. (2020) Computing with CodeRunner at Coventry University: Automated summative assessment of Python and C++ code. In Proceedings of the 4th Conference on Computing Education Practice 2020 (pp. 1-4).

GitHub Classroom, Accessed 26 June 2022, <https://docs.github.com/en/education/quickstart>

H5P, Accessed 26 June 2022, <htttps://h5p.org/>

Johnson, R.D., Hornik, S. and Salas, E. (2008) An empirical examination of factors contributing to the creation of successful e-learning environments, International Journal of Human-Computer Studies, Volume 66, Issue 5, Pages 356-369, ISSN 1071-5819, https://doi.org/10.1016/j.ijhcs.2007.11.003.

Kurniawati, A., Kusumaningsih, A., Sophan, M. K. (2018) Visualization code tools for teaching and learning introductory programming. In 2018 2nd International Conference on Informatics for Development (ICID) (pp. 97-100).

Lobb, R. and Harlow, J. (2016) Coderunner: A tool for assessing computer programming skills. ACM Inroads, 7(1), 47-51.

Mahdizadeh, H., Biemans, H. and Mulder, M. (2008) Determining factors of the use of e-learning environments by university teachers, Computers Education, Volume 51, Issue 1, Pages 142-154, ISSN 0360-1315, https://doi.org/10.1016/j.compedu.2007.04.004.

Moore, J.L., Dickson-Deane, C. and Galyen, K. (2011) e-Learning, online learning, and distance learning environments: Are they the same? The Internet and Higher

Education, Volume 14, Issue 2, Pages 129-135, ISSN 1096- 7516, https://doi.org/10.1016/j.iheduc.2010.10.001.

National IT-BPM Workforce Survey - ICTA 2019, Accessed 26 June 2022, <https://www.icta.lk/projects/national-it-bpm-workforce-survey-2019/>

National Policy Framework Vistas of Prosperity and Splendour 2019, Accessed 06 July 2022, <http://www.doc.gov.lk/images/pdf/NationalPolicyframeworkEN/FinalDovVer02-English.pdf>

Parkes, M., Stein, S. and Reading, C. (2015) Student preparedness for university e learning environments, The Internet and Higher Education, Volume 25, Pages 1-10, ISSN 1096-7516, https://doi.org/10.1016/j.iheduc.2014.10.002.

Author Biographies

Mrs Vishaka Nanayakkara: Senior Lecturer at the Department of Computer Science & Engineering and the Director of the Centre for Open and Distance Learning (CODL), University of Moratuwa. She is also a board director at ICT Agency (ICTA) of Sri Lanka.

Dr Buddhika Karunarathne: Senior Lecturer at the Department of Computer Science & Engineering, University of Moratuwa

Prof Malik Ranasinghe: Professor at the Department of Civil Engineering, University of Moratuwa and the Chairman of The Information and Communication Technology Agency (ICTA), Sri Lanka.

Dr Amal Shehan Perera: Senior Lecturer at the Department of Computer Science & Engineering, University of Moratuwa and the Director of the Centre for Information Technology Services (CITeS), University of Moratuwa Sri Lanka.

Other contributors

Dr Gayashan Amarasinghe: Senior Lecturer at the Department of Computer Science & Engineering, University of Moratuwa

Dr Sandareka Wickramanayake: Lecturer at the Department of Computer Science & Engineering, University of Moratuwa

Dr Supunmali Ahangama: Senior Lecturer at the Department of Information Technology, University of Moratuwa

Dr Kulani Mahadewa: Senior Lecturer at the Department of Information Technology, University of Moratuwa

Dr Chathuranga Hettiarachchi: Senior Lecturer at the Department of Computer Science & Engineering, University of Moratuwa

Mr Hasith Yaggahavita: CTO - 99X, Co-Founder - IgniterSpace, Co-Founder - Maturify, Chief Disruption Officer - StartupX Foundary.

Teachers in Action: Producing, Differentiating and Digitalizing Content Lesson Materials for Inclusive Lessons in Grades 4 and 5

Lisa Paleczek[1,3], Daniela Ender[1,2,3], Jessica Berger[1,3], David Wohlhart[3,4], Lorenz Kern[4]

[1] University of Graz, Austria
[2] Private University College of Teacher Education Augustinum, Graz, Austria
[3] Research Center for Inclusive Education, Graz, Austria
[4] Wohlhart Lernsoftware, Graz, Austria

lisa.paleczek@uni-graz.at
daniela.ender@uni-graz.at
jessica.berger@uni-graz.at
david@wohlhart.at
lkern@wohlhart.at

Abstract The present case study deals with the development of an editor application for digitalizing content material at different reading levels in the project ReginaDiff (Regional, Sustainable and Differentiated in classroom. Starting the green transformation in school). The editor allows texts to be adapted by enabling the insertion of text passages, pictures, glossary words and various reading tasks that have been shown to support reading comprehension in students. In order to investigate the editor's practicality and user-friendliness, we conducted a survey, employing interviews and questionnaires, of 12 teachers who had used the new editor to create digital materials in teacher training sessions. During the training sessions provided, teachers began by inserting the text passages at the highest reading level, then highlighted the glossary words (together with pictures and written as well as audio explanations) and also added exercises from a selection of eight possible exercise types. They then transferred this highest level to the other reading levels for appropriate adaptation. The teachers liked using the editor and found it to be user-friendly. Most teachers found the digitalization of exercises, glossary words and pictures, etc. to be quite intuitive. Even though most teachers reported having initial difficulties, they also stated that working with the editor became easier as they gained familiarity with its functions and possibilities.

Introduction

The ability to read is a fundamental prerequisite for learning in all subject areas and, when viewed in a wider context, for general participation in society. Several elements have been shown to foster reading abilities and text comprehension in students: vocabulary work (National Reading Panel, 2000), reading strategies (McNamara, 2007), cooperative learning (Hattie and Ziehrer, 2019), providing texts matching students' reading abilities (differentiation: Förster, Kawohl and Souvignier, 2019) and reading comprehension exercises, which also provide teachers with the opportunity to assess students' reading comprehension. Digitalization helps provide such elements when working with a diverse body of students. In the project RegiNaDiff (Regional, Sustainable and Differentiated in classroom. Starting the green transformation in school), these elements are joint in a digital learning environment providing reading material for different lessons at school.

In the predecessor project RegioDiff (Discovering regions of Styria: differentiated materials for inclusive content lessons in Grade 4; Paleczek, 2020), we successfully developed content lesson materials consisting of texts and corresponding tasks that incorporate the previously mentioned elements in a digitalized learning environment. The usability of this digital learning environment and the concept were piloted in a usability and feasibility study (Paleczek, Ender, Berger, Prinz and Seifert, 2022). Teachers and students liked the material and found the learning environment to be intuitive. Teachers stated that they would like to have more different topics that are implemented in the digital learning environment to use it in various lessons with their students. Hence, in order to provide teachers with the possibility of creating their own content materials following the RegioDiff-framework, we started the successor project RegiNaDiff. In this project, we developed an editor application for teachers that enables them to digitalize differentiated material for implementation in inclusive Grade 4 and 5 classrooms. This editor was then piloted in teacher training sessions that accompanied the teachers as they created and differentiated the material, digitalized it and then used it in their classrooms.

In this paper, we present the initial results on how the teachers experienced working with this editor application. To investigate usability and user-friendliness, we conducted interviews and questionnaires with 12 teachers who had created digital materials using the editor. While the initial results corroborate the editor's general usability, some adjustments will still be necessary to enhance functionality and ease and scope of use.

Developing the RegiNaDiff editor

In theory, teachers have the possibility of developing differentiated reading tasks within all available advanced learning management systems. In practice, however, owing to the lack of pre-configured templates and ready-made models and didactical support concerning task type, task structure, sequencing of the tasks, etc., this is only possible when teachers possess both highly developed media and didactical knowledge. We developed our RegiNaDiff-editor as a response to this unsatisfactory state of affairs.

The editor aims at offering a simple and clear user interface that leads through all the steps necessary to develop differentiated digital reading material based on text passages and corresponding tasks (Figure 1).

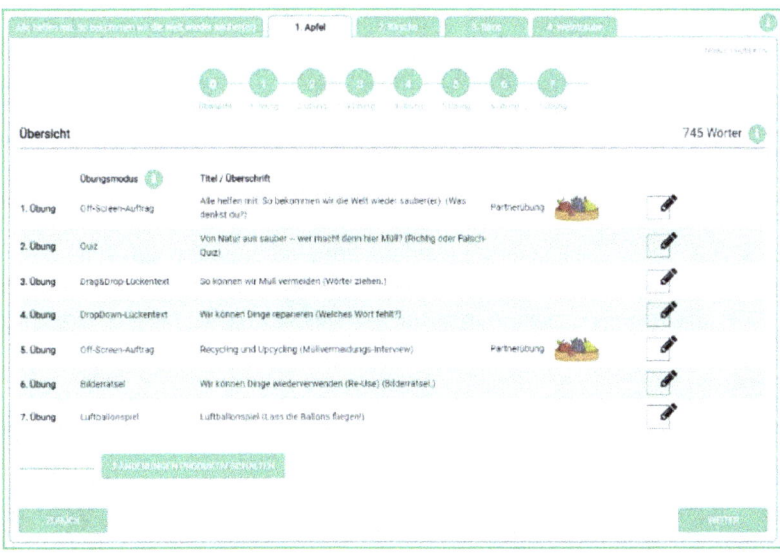

Figure 1: Editor's user interface in the overview for seven reading passages and corresponding tasks.

This user interface enables teachers (a) to add reading passages with pictures, (b) to highlight difficult words in these reading passages and thereby define via pop-up certain glossary words that can be coupled with written and audio explanations and/or illustrations (see Figure 2), and (c) to create different tasks corresponding to the reading passages.

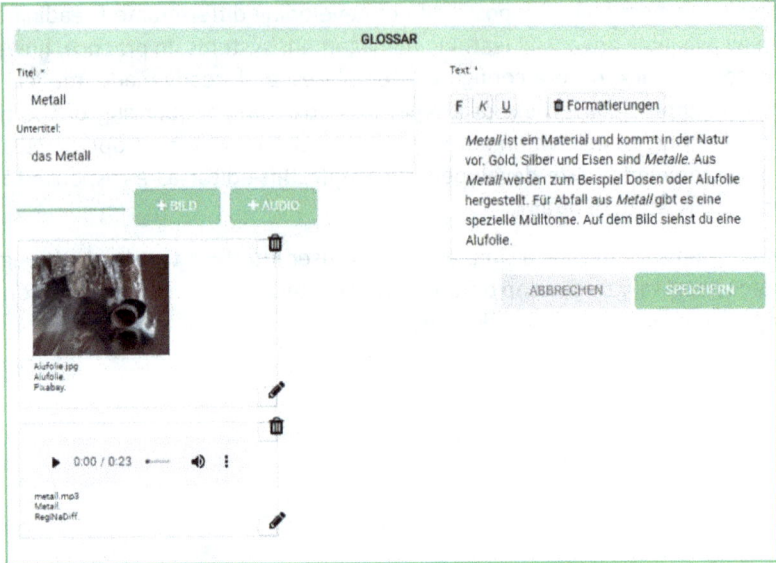

Figure 2: Defining and explaining a glossary word in the editor. Left side: the word, the word with the article (a German peculiarity of nouns), picture, audio. Right side: the written explanation of the glossary word with the glossary word itself in italics.

Tasks that are to be worked on in pairs are highlighted by a fruit basket. The fruit basket was chosen because each difficulty level in the material is named after a regional fruit (apple, cherry, pear, grape).

The task types (Figures 3-10) are based on evidence-based templates that had proven successful in the previous project. Each topic starts and ends with a certain task type to provide a certain routine for the students. The instructions for the different task types are pre-defined (this is also to provide students with a routine) and teachers can look them up in a step-by-step instruction booklet on the digitalization process that the project team prepared (Ender, Berger and Paleczek, 2022). There are eight different task types that teachers can employ:

- **Off-screen task:** requires use of exercise books and/or pair discussion. This task type is used for cooperative learning and reading strategy training tasks (Figure 3). In a combination of reading strategy and cooperative learning task, it is always used as the first exercise before students start to read the text. They are asked to individually predict what the text will be about based on the headline. Then, students share it in pairs and present the result to the class (Figure 3). This exercise is based on the think-pair-share concept of cooperative learning methods (Brüning and Saum, 2006; Lyman 1981) as well as on predicting the content as a reading strategy training (Cromley and Azevedo, 2007; McNemara, 2007).

- **Quiz:** answering questions/statements on the reading passage (yes/no; true/false) (Figure 4). This is a typical exercise to assess if the students have read and understood the text passage. This type of question is also used in reading comprehension tests (e.g., Salzburger Lesescreening: Mayringer and Wimmer, 2014).
- **Drag & drop gap text:** filling in the gaps in sentences by selecting items from words provided (Figure 5). Each word provided is to be used for filling one of the gaps, hence, the number of words and gaps matches.
- **Drop down gap text**: selecting the correct item out of three words provided (Figure 6). The two words provided that are not the right words are used to distract the students. It is important that they would make sense grammatically, however, do not fit the content read before.
- **Make a list**: matching words to certain categories that have been described in the text passage. For instance, there could be a list for food of animal-origin and one for food of plant-origin (Figure 7). As in all the tasks, the information to solve the exercise needs to be provided in the text to make sure the task does not assess knowledge but reading comprehension.
- **Picture puzzle:** matching words and pictures (Figure 8). The words can either represent the name of the item on the picture (this would be suitable for weaker readers) or be otherwise related to the picture like a sentence of written explanation (this would be suitable for stronger readers).
- **Memory game:** matching words and pictures (Figure 9). In the students' view, this task is played like the well-known "Memory-game" in German speaking countries. Students have to turn over face down cards to find two cards that match.
- **Balloon game:** guessing a word that is the answer to a question based on the information provided in the text by adding letters (Figure 10). Each wrong decision makes a balloon burst. This exercise is always the last exercise of the topic to sum up the content and to add a playful moment in the material.

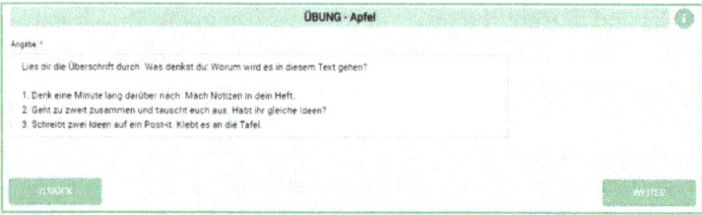

Figure 3: Example for an off-screen task: reading strategy exercise combined with cooperative learning elements as the 1st exercise of each text to provide students with a routine.

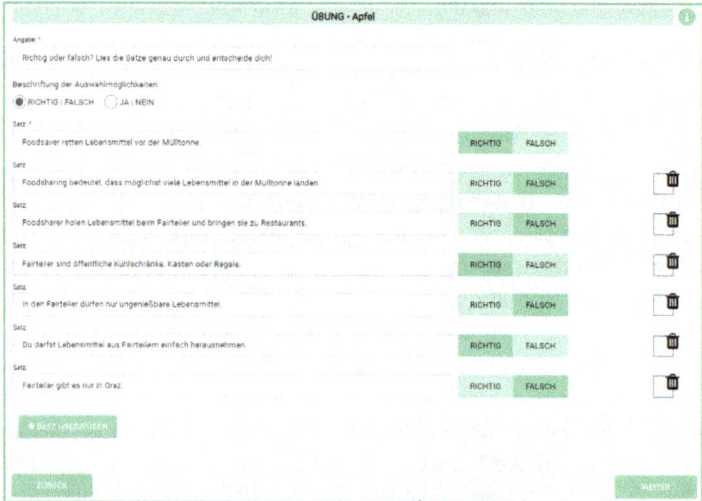

Figure 4: Quiz on a reading passage. Statements are presented and students need to decide whether they are true or false based on the text passage that they read before. In the editor you can switch to the yes/no-format for students to answer question by simply clicking on Ja/Nein (upper part of the figure).

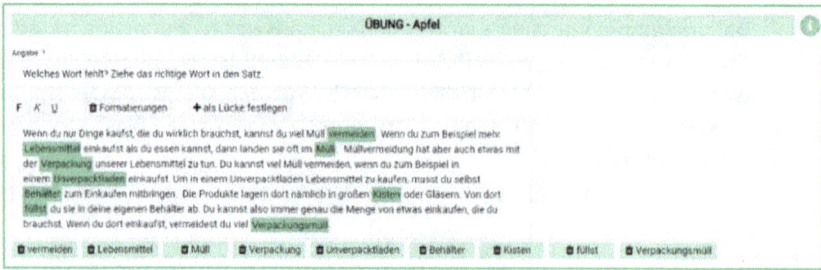

Figure 5: Gap text (drag and drop task). The words marked in green will be shown as gaps in the text ad students need to drag and drop the words presented in boxes to the fitting gap.

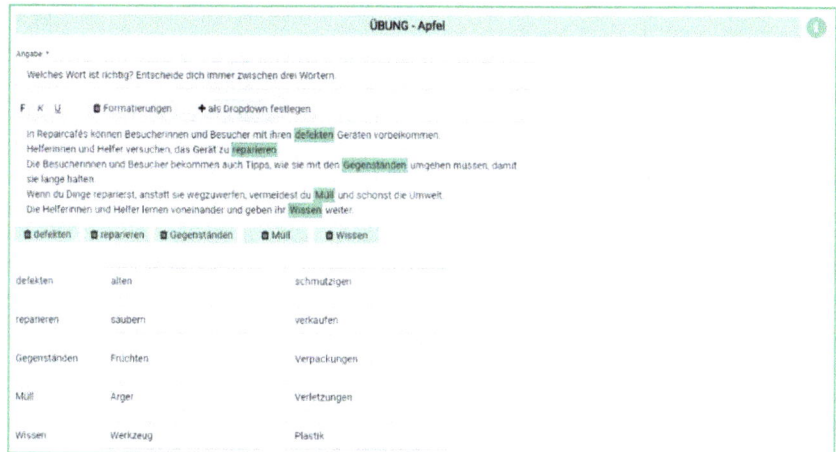

Figure 6: Gap text (dropdown menu). The words marked in green in the text represent the correct solution. For each word, two more words have to be defined as distractors (see lower part of the figure) that make sense in terms of grammar but do not represent the right solution.

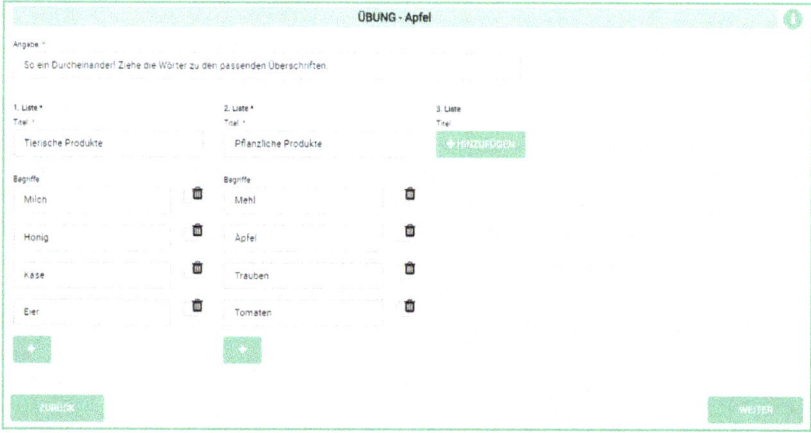

Figure 7: Make a list with two lists (animal- and plant-origin products) and four items each.

Figure 8: Picture puzzle with different trash cans and some examples for materials that belong in each.

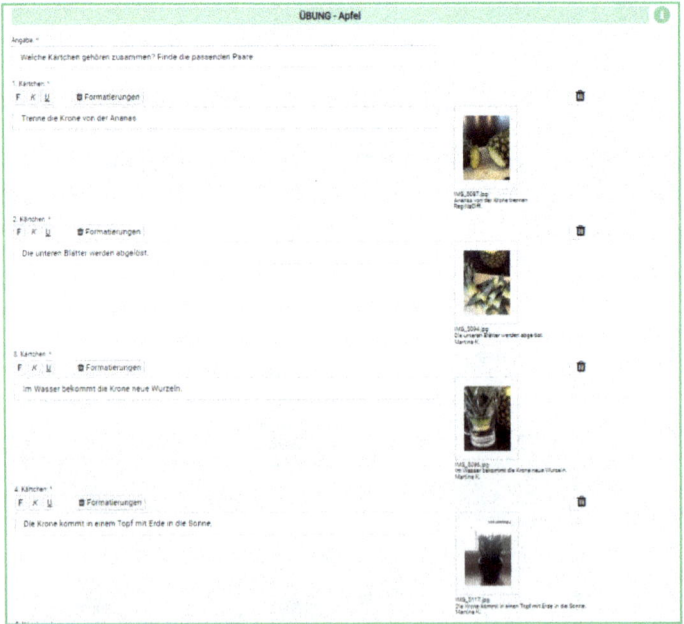

Figure 9: Memory game with pictures and written information on how to grow a pineapple plant.

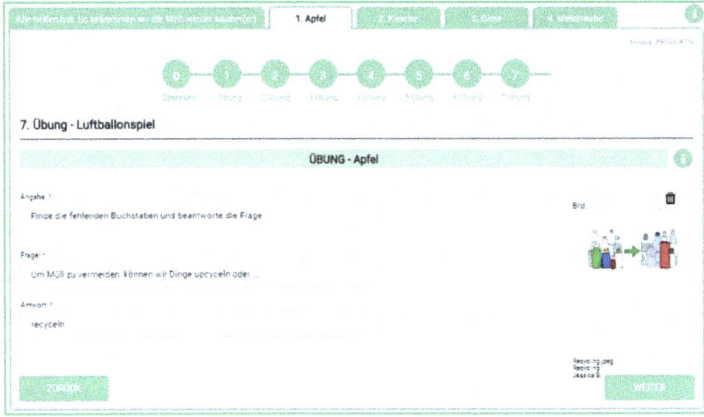

Figure 10: Balloon game, which is the last exercise of each topic.

The editor automatically counts the number of words in all reading passages (red box in Figure 11).

In the initial phase, teachers are required to start with the most difficult level which is characterized by an apple. This level consists of about 750 words accounting for all reading passages but not the tasks. Teachers are required to put together a suitable sequence of tasks for this level, one task per reading passage. A step-by-step-instruction booklet for teachers on how to write and differentiate reading texts and on which tasks they can employ (Berger, Ender and Paleczek, 2022) as well as info-buttons within the editor (red box in Figure 12) provide additional support in creating the text passages and the tasks.

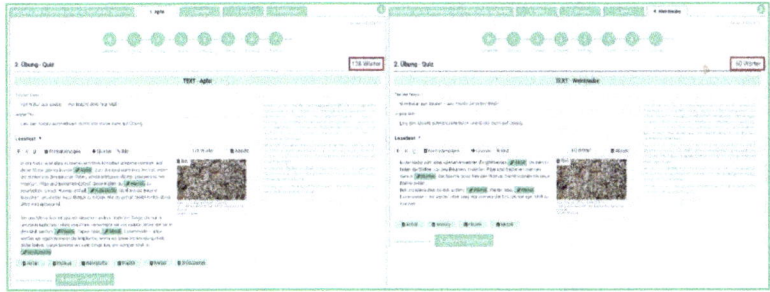

Figure 11: Word count for the second reading passage at the most (apple) and least difficult (grape) differentiation level (see red box). Words marked in green are glossary words.

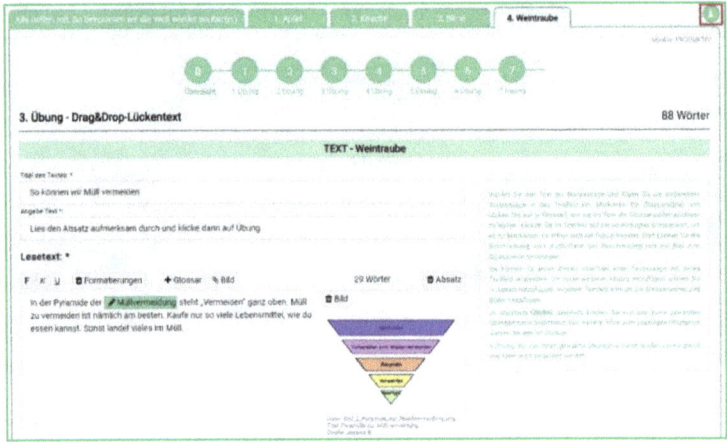

Figure 12: Info-button for the different modes (design, adapt, productive, public) (see red box).

The editor uses a total of four different work modes: design, adapt, productive and public. As mentioned above, teachers have to start creating the most difficult level. They write the text passages (level 1 / apple: 750 words in total) and create the corresponding tasks. After finishing the most difficult level (Mode 1: design), the content is copied to the other three differentiation levels (level 2 / cherry: 550 words; level 3 / pear: 350 words; level 4 / grape: 250 words). Working through these other levels (Mode 2: adapt), teachers reduce the complexity of the text passages, add, or delete glossary words, and reduce gaps or items in all tasks or adapt the tasks corresponding to the differentiated content. In this step, it is crucial that teachers check if all the information needed for solving the tasks is still available in the text passage as they had been shortened in the differentiation process. After the project team had corrected the four differentiation levels (texts and corresponding tasks) between the teacher training sessions, teachers could make their differentiated bundle of texts and tasks available to their classroom (Mode 3: productive) and to other users on the platform (Mode 4: public). In Mode 4, all participating teachers could choose out of the available texts.

With these different functions and in combination with the accompanying teacher training, the editor enables teachers to (a) digitally create reading texts and corresponding sequences of evidence-based reading tasks on four levels of differentiation, (b) make use of the texts and tasks in their inclusive classrooms, while (c) easily keeping track of the students' learning results within a digital learning environment.

Aims and research questions

Since the editor was developed based on the concept of the RegioDiff-project, we knew which elements of the digital material would work in the digital learning environment when working with the material in a classroom. What we did not know, however, was whether the editor application had all the necessary functions to produce this kind of material and whether it was easy to handle for the teachers. Therefore, we wanted to learn more about the editor's practicality as well as user-friendliness to benefit from the teachers' experiences while working with the editor in order to adapt or add functions, if necessary.

Method

To investigate the above-mentioned research interests, we employed a mixed-methods approach using a questionnaire and interviewed the teachers who participated in the teacher training accompanying their text and task production, differentiation and digitalization. The teacher training took place in spring 2022 and the teachers worked in pairs producing, differentiating, enriching and digitalizing texts and tasks.

Sample

The sample consisted of 11 female and one male teacher(s) (4 in secondary school, 7 in primary school, 1 in both) aged 24 to 59 (M=31, SD=10.99) who participated in the RegiNaDiff teacher training sessions (3 afternoons) on how to create, digitalize and implement differentiated material. The individual level of teaching experience varied from 6 months to 35 years (M=6.38; SD=10.72).

Instruments

1. *Questionnaire*

For this study, we conducted an online questionnaire before the last training afternoon (April 2022) in order to collect teacher feedback on working with the editor. The questionnaire items consisted of single choice questions, five-point Likert scales from 1 (not at all true) to 5 (completely true) and open questions. For example, teachers had to rate several statements on working with the editor (e.g., "Working with the editor was intuitive."; "I found all functions I needed."; "The structure of the editor was easy to understand."; "I am satisfied with the functions provided by the editor."), how they experienced the digitalization process of the texts, tasks and glossary words using the editor (e.g., "I knew exactly which tasks to select in the editor."; "The differentiation process in the editor was easy for me."; "The creation of the glossary words was intuitive."; "Creating the tasks was easy for me.") and the feedback and support provided by the project team (e.g., "The support provided by the project team was sufficient.").

2. Interviews

After teachers had digitalized their differentiated reading materials (texts and tasks), we then conducted a semi-structured interview with them in April and May 2022. The interview guideline was structured around the following topics: (1) personal experience and attitude towards digital differentiated materials (e.g., "How often do you use differentiated materials in your lessons?"), (2) producing the RegiNaDiff-materials on their own (e.g., "How did you feel about writing the text?"; "Could you briefly describe the process?"), (3) pre-experience with digital devices and media (e.g., "What digital media do you use in class?"), (4) digitalization and the use of the editor (e.g., "How was working with the editor for you?"; "How satisfied are you with the design options in the editor?"), (5) the upcoming implementation of their texts in class (e.g., "Do you think the differentiated digital texts will be suitable for all students in your class?"), and (6) the evaluation of their work ("On a scale of 1 to 10, how satisfied are you with the result?").

For the purposes of the present paper, it was of major interest for us to investigate the digitalization of the material (including texts, written and audio-recorded glossary words, pictures, and tasks), and the perceived advantages and disadvantages of using digitalized, differentiated materials for teachers and students.

In total, we had 8.23 hours of interview material.

Results

Eleven (92%) of the twelve teachers had never worked with an editor before they joined the RegiNaDiff-project. Nonetheless, a large proportion of the group described working with the editor as very easy (N=2; 17%) or easy (N=6; 50%). The teachers described working with the editor as very intuitive (N=4; 33%), intuitive (N=4; 33%) and partly intuitive (N=3; 25%). In total, ten teachers either fully agreed (N=5; 42%) or agreed (N=5; 42%) that they had been able to find all the functions they needed. However, the interviews also revealed that almost all teachers reported having had initial difficulties. In contrast, one teacher had "assumed it to be more difficult. It worked out better than I imagined" (teacher 05.4; #00:30:08).

Most teachers reported positively regarding editor **user-friendliness** ("Yes, well, I think it was possible to orient oneself" teacher 02.1b; #00:27:21) and the functions "were easy to find" (teacher 01.1a; #00:45:49). For others, working with the editor became more intuitive as they developed familiarity with the functions and possibilities the editor offered. After spending some time finding their feet, the initial uncertainty was dissipated through a process of trial and error. Here, the use of the step-by-step-instruction booklet was described as being "extremely important" (teacher 02.1b; #00:29:24). As one teacher put it: "I would like to have it at hand at a second or third time too" (teacher 02.1b; #00:29:24). Some teachers also mentioned that the use of the editor was not self-explanatory: "I don't think I could do this without the instruction[booklet]" (teacher 07.4b; #00:49:50). As one teacher stated: "if you are a part of the teacher training and you have the documents, it is super user-friendly, but I would say to digitalize something without this extra instruction or the print version that already existed at this point, it would have been more difficult, but possible" (teacher 01.1a, #00:49:11).

Ten of the teachers responded in the questionnaire that they had used the **information-buttons** for additional support in the digitalization process, and that they had found them helpful. In line with this, in the interviews, most teachers said that the info buttons were helpful for orientation within the editor. Some teachers mentioned that they had not found the buttons helpful or that they simply had not used them because they knew what to do anyway. In general, they found the editor to be very easy to understand (N=5; 42%) or easy to understand (N=5; 42%).

Ten teachers digitalized **glossary words** and reported finding it very easy (N=6; 60%), easy (N=2; 20%) or not easy at all (N=2; 20%). The two teachers who had difficulties with the editor found that digitalization of the glossary words was not intuitive at all, while those who found it to be very easy or easy also experienced it as being very intuitive (N=6; 60%) or intuitive (N=2; 20%). One teacher found glossary work very frustrating because the upload did not work. After the highest difficulty level had been transferred to the other differentiation levels, some teachers then found it difficult to have to change glossary words in each level by hand. More details on the various steps in digitalizing the glossary are presented in Table 1.

Table 1: Teachers' perceptions concerning digitalizing glossary words and audio files and images

	very intuitive	intuitive	partly intuitive	rather unintuitive	not intuitive at all
digitalizing glossary words	N=6	N=2	N=0	N=0	N=2
uploading audio files	N=4	N=1	N=3	N=1	N=1
uploading images/pictures	N=4	N=1	N=3	N=1	N=1

Nine teachers **created digital tasks** in the editor. They described it as being very easy (N=3; 33%) or easy (N=3; 33%). In the interviews, some teachers mentioned that the only difficulty was that you had to create each type of task at least once in order to understand how it was done and to become familiar with the procedures required. After that, they experienced it as being easy.

The interviews revealed that teachers found dealing with mistakes to be quite frustrating: "this was difficult to figure out how to undo clicks, how to get back, when something went wrong" (teacher 02.1b; #00:27:27). For example, this included deleting a glossary word by accident (which then requires re-creation of the glossary word) or correcting erroneous task sequencing. Once initial editor positions had been set, the position could not be changed. Additionally, the position in the sequence was copied to the other differentiation levels. This meant that teachers then had to change it by hand in every level.

Seven teachers **uploaded pictures** to the text. They found it to be very easy (N=4; 57%) or easy (N=1; 14%). On the whole, it was found to be very intuitive (N=2; 29%) or intuitive (N=3; 42%). Teachers also perceived labelling the pictures as being very intuitive (N=3; 43%), intuitive (N=3; 43%) or partly intuitive (N=1; 14%). The interviews provided us with valuable information on where exactly the teachers experienced difficulties. For example, when they forgot to first insert a picture and then copied the first differentiation level to all the other levels, they then had to insert the picture by hand at each level.

Ten teachers **differentiated the materials in the editor**, three experienced it as very easy (30%) and seven as easy (70%). For the most part, they reported that it was very convenient (N=7; 70%) or convenient (N=2; 20%) that the editor automatically copied the information from the most difficult level to all the other levels. Despite this, teachers largely found the adaptation of the levels to be very (N=3; 30%) or partly tedious (N=4; 40%).

Concerning the different **editing modes** (design, adapt, productive, public), the teachers described them as very comprehensible (N=6; 50%) or comprehensible (N=5; 42%). Two thirds of the teachers stated that they were very satisfied (N=2; 17%) or satisfied (N=7; 58%) with the various options the editor provided.

In general, the teachers reported being very satisfied with the **support of the project team** during the digitalization process. Nine teachers experienced it as being very important (75%), two as important (17%) and one as partly important (8%). Additionally, nine teachers fully agreed (75%) and three teachers agreed (25%) that they had received enough support. The feedback provided by the project team was perceived as positive and respectful. 83% (N=10) of the teachers were very satisfied (N=6; 50%) or satisfied (N=4; 33%) with the guidance provided during the teacher training sessions.

Half of the teachers said that they would like to **digitalize further materials using the editor**. Among the reasons given by teachers for not wanting to create further digital materials were a general preference for analogue materials, and the view that the digitalization of materials was very time-consuming. Some teachers recommended adaptations of the editor such as providing the opportunity to undo clicks and more freedom to change things instead of having to stick rigidly to the given structure. When asked why they thought new materials needed to be developed, they mentioned the increasing importance of digital and differentiated materials. They also expressed the view that digitalization of materials provided more scope in addressing different topics which the students could then work on more autonomously. One teacher stated that working with the editor was fun. In general, the teachers said that using the editor a second time would be easier now that they had become familiar with its functions and with the possibilities it provided. Some teachers stated that they would like to write and digitalize texts in a more simplified form (e.g., with no glossary words, and no differentiation into four different levels). To ease working with the editor and to make it more intuitive and user-friendly, teachers wished for more options when uploading pictures and the possibility of copying a changed glossary word into all other differentiation levels using one click.

The teachers reported that the use of digital devices was very attractive for the students. Nevertheless, they still appreciated the use of offscreen activities, interactive discussion and co-operation in real-life-settings, and the use of exercises or books in paper format ("to grab a book has also its values, it's really important" teacher 02.1b; #00:20:55). In their opinion the mixture of digital and print materials provided by the editor is a good, workable combination for classroom practice.

Discussion and future steps

In general, there appear to be no barriers to successful implementation of the editor in its current form within the RegiNaDiff-project environment. While we drew on teacher feedback to make several necessary adaptations to the editor, some shortcomings still need to be addressed in future developments.

The teachers identified the one-to-one copying of the complete task sequence to simpler levels as being a limitation in practice. This procedure is based on the original decision to enable presentation of identical tasks to the whole inclusive classroom, followed by the possibility of differentiating them with respect to the required levels of reading competence. Nevertheless, after reflecting on feedback, it would seem that as the task types themselves may require different sets of competencies from students, it may also be desirable to allow for changing the task types individually at each level. Furthermore, additional task types could be useful in the classroom. For instance, it could be practical to offer a task providing four different answers (one right answer and three distractors) to a question asked instead of just choosing between yes and no or true and false.

Currently, most of the implemented task types are based on closed questions where the students only can choose between a set of proposed answers. An extension would be open tasks, especially with the possibility for students to post their results in the form of pictures and videos made with their smartphones. Other students could be given the opportunity to comment and like each other's results, thus adding a social and gamification component to learning.

A further limitation is that, currently, the text reading levels are checked using an external tool, RATTE (Wild and Pissarek, n.d.). Integrating such a tool into the editor would be very helpful. One possible candidate for such an integrated checking tool is an ongoing development by capito digital (Fröhlich, Candussi and Bucht, 2021). This new tool is capable of checking the language level used, marking problematic words, and, at a more advanced level, of suggesting "translation" into simpler language and structures that could be transferred to the easier levels. This would further facilitate the differentiation processes for teachers.

To successfully produce and digitalize the RegiNaDiff-materials, we offered support for the teachers in various ways. The teacher training was necessary and the teachers appreciated the support provided within the training sessions. Yet, the project team also provided a lot of support in between the sessions and helped with close supervision. Teachers could send emails or call members of the project team whenever questions appeared. The members of the project team corrected all texts and tasks to fit in the project concept. Additionally, the teachers had the step-by-step instructions to guide them through the text and task production as well as the differentiation and digitalization. These support offers were necessary since we had not known then whether the editor worked with all the functions planned and whether the teachers found it intuitive or not. Since we know not, further steps can be taken to make the pool of texts grow and to enable teachers to independently produce texts. In a next step, the support measures would need to be reduced because there will not be the opportunity to provide this kind of support outside the project.

Finally, the editor described here was developed for a specific proprietary learning management system. To enable use on a broader level, plugins for freely available learning management systems could also be developed.

References

Berger, J., Ender, D. and Paleczek, L. (2022) "Manual zur Erstellung von differenzierten Sachtexten in RegioDiff und RegiNaDiff." https://static.uni-graz.at/fileadmin/projekte/regional-nachhaltig-differenziert/Manual_Texterstellung/Manual_Texterstellung_RegioUndRegiNa_fuer_Homepage_Final.pdf

Brüning, L. and Saum, T. (2006) "Erfolgreich unterrichten durch Kooperatives Lernen. Strategien zur Schüleraktivierung", Neue Deutsche Schule Verlagsgesellschaft, Essen.

Cromley, J. G. and Azevedo, R. (2007) "Self-report of reading comprehension strategies: What are we measuring?", Metacognition and Learning, 1(3), 229–247. https://doi.org/10.1007/s11409-006-9002-5

Ender, D., Berger, J. and Paleczek, L. (2022) "Manual zur Digitalisierung differenzierter Sachtexte im Projekt RegiNaDiff." https://static.uni-graz.at/fileadmin/projekte/regional-nachhaltig-differenziert/Manual_Digitalisierung/Manual_Digitalisierung.pdf

Mayringer, H. and Wimmer, H. (2014) "SLS 2-9: Salzburger Lese-Screening für die Schulstufen 2-9. " Hogrefe, Göttingen.

Paleczek, L., Ender, D., Berger, J., Prinz, K., & Seifert, S. (2022) "A feasibility study of digital content use in inclusive, Austrian primary school practice." *International Journal of Educational Research*, 112. https://doi.org/10.1016/j.ijer.2022.101938

Paleczek, L. (2020) "How to Produce and Acquire Regional Knowledge Digitally and in Print: Conceptualisation of the RegioDiff-Project." In C. Busch, M. Steinicke, & T. Wendler (Chairs), Proceedings of the 19th European Conference on e-Learning: A Virtual Conference hosted by University of Applied Sciences HTW Berlin, Germany, Online, 611-614.

Förster, N., Kawohl, E. and Souvignier, E. (2018) "Short- and long-term effects of assessment-based differentiated reading instruction in general education on reading fluency and reading comprehension", *Learning and Instruction*, Vol 56, pp 98-109, https://doi.org/10.1016/j.learninstruc.2018.04.009.

Fröhlich, W., Candussi, K. and Bucht, E. (2021) "Wirkungsorientierter Geschäftsbericht nach dem Social Reporting Standard", [online], Graz: atempo, https://www.capito.eu/wp-content/uploads/sites/3/Online_Wirkungsbericht-2020_capito_V4.pdf.

Hattie, J. and Zierer, K. (2019) *Visible learning insights*. Routledge, Abingdon Oxon, New York NY, https://doi.org/10.4324/9781351002226.

Lyman, F.T. (1981) "The responsive classroom discussion: The inclusion of all students". In A. Anderson (Ed.), Mainstreaming Digest (109-113), University of Maryland Press, College Park.

McNamara, D. S. (Ed.) (2007) *Reading comprehension strategies: Theories, interventions, and technologies*, Lawrence Erlbaum Associates, New Jersey.

National Reading Panel (NRP) (2000) "Teaching Children to Read: An Evidence-Based Assessment of the Scientific Research Literature on Reading and Its Implications for

Reading Instruction", Rockville MD: National Institute of Child Health and Human Development.

Wild, J. and Pissarek, M. (n.d.) "Ratte. Regensburger Analysetool für Texte. Version 1.6.1.", [online], www.uni-regensburg.de/sprache-literatur-kultur/germanistik-did/downloads/ratte/index.html.

Author Biograhies

Lisa Paleczek, PhD is an assistant-professor at the University of Graz at the Inclusive Education Unit. Her research focuses on inclusive classroom practices, digital tools to ease differentiation and assessment. In her current project, digital assessment tools and digital learning environments and materials for primary school students are developed and evaluated.

Daniela Ender is a researcher at the Private University College for Teacher Education and the University of Graz. She is a team-member at the Research Center for Inclusive Education and PhD candidate at the University of Graz. Her research interests are the differentiation and digitalization of reading materials for primary school students.

Jessica Berger, BA MSc, is currently doing her PhD in Inclusive Education at the University of Graz and is a predoctoral researcher at the Research Center for Inclusive Education (University of Graz). Her research is on Open Educational Resources (OER) with a special focus on their inclusive use in schools.

David Wohlhart is a teacher in schools for children with special needs, in inclusive classes in primary and secondary schools, professor at universities and teacher training colleges, author of coursebooks, founder and CEO of Wohlhart-Lernsoftware GmbH.

Lorenz Kernholds a BEd in information and communication pedagogics. Instructor for different sports, lecturer of first aid for red cross Austria. Head developer of RegioDiff & RegiNaDiff. He is a junior developer & system operator in training at Wohlhart-Lernsoftware GmbH

Using e-Learning to Support Entrepreneurs at a Time of Crisis: A South African perspective

Sweta Patnaik[1] and Shamil Isaacs[2]
[1]Dept of Clothing and Textile Technology
[2]Technology Station Clothing and Textiles
Cape Peninsula University of Technology, Cape Town, South Africa
patnaiks@cput.ac.za[1] and isaacssh@cput.ac.za[2]

Abstract: The pandemic has left many new and existing entrepreneurs in the clothing manufacturing industry at a 'blind-alley'. On the other end, there are many left over off cuts and swatches disposed of by manufacturing units and retailers that could be otherwise given a meaningful purpose to contribute towards minimizing waste and supporting the circular economy. This will prevent environmental pollution in many ways and contribute towards a sustainable world. While web-based interventions have been the highlight for many years, especially since the COVID-19 pandemic, we thought of bringing this into the world of the less privileged where survivalist entrepreneurs, Small Medium and Micro Enterprises (SMEs) and the unemployed can benefit. South Africa is currently facing high rate of unemployment; therefore, this effort is to slightly minimize this and contribute towards employment and skill building. We through our final year diploma students at the Department of Clothing and Textile Technology at Cape Peninsula University of Technology presented the concept of an entrepreneurial hub. The project involved creating waste minimizing creative artefacts in various forms. There were multilingual digital storytelling videos on the most commonly spoken regional language of South Africa. The videos were compressed and images were sourced for low tech accessibility. They were made available via YouTube and WhatsApp keeping the data constraint and ease of access in mind. The project currently has no cost involved to any party, yet earn new skill sets and provide a source of income during these difficult times. The goal is to transform the primary idea that people have; unidimensional understanding of what sustainability comprises of and not how it could have a multidimensional impact to the society, environment and improve the quality of life. There has been a lot of interest from the community and retail clothing industry offering support. The approach to the impact have been multimodal with pre and post surveys, focus group interviews with entrepreneurs and small businesses. Feedback has been positive with people highlighting the need for such a change in South Africa and the culmination of such a platform where unemployment could be minimised. A qualitative study with key role players indicated the need for a formal free and open access platform that needs to be made available and we are in discussion at the institutional level. Further research will include establishing an entrepreneurial hub to ensure access to stakeholders with lab equipment funded by the department and the technology station.

Introduction

COVID-19 has gained a lot of attention from scholars for the impact it has on entrepreneurship in general (Kuckertz & Brandle, 2021; Syriopoulos, 2020; Gregurec et al., 2021). Empirical evidence boasts that entrepreneurship, and particularly SMEs, can easily identify and make profit-oriented changes in the market (Syriopoulos, 2020). As a result of the pandemic, the entrepreneurs have been faced with unforeseen transitions in all facets of entrepreneurial works, like changes in market patterns, demand from consumers, and introduction of new policies to contain the proliferation of the COVID-19 virus (Kuckertz & Brandle, 2021; Gregurec et al., 2021). Technological experts said the COVID-19 virus as a global disruption which can either prove to be an opportunity or challenge to the existing business models through implementing new technologies to support business processes (Gregurec et al., 2021). The pandemic in general resulted in an increase in entrepreneurial activities across the globe, more so in biotech firms (Cancherini et al., 2021). Evidence highlights that there was no wide application of technology by SMEs in the past years, however due to the COVID-19 disruptions they have adopted use of digital technologies to avoid shutting down (Gregurec et al., 2021).

While the pandemic seems to provide entrepreneurial opportunities, the then ongoing lockdowns in different parts of the world have led to slowed entrepreneurial activity, mostly being the closure of ventures. This view is supported by Alessa, et al. (2021) who report that due to the impact of COVID-19, SMEs have been forced to shut down. In addition, there has been a sharp decrease in consumer demand due to the consumer's inability either to visit stores to purchase basic necessities or cash shortages. SMEs cannot exist in vacuum; they exist and survive in entrepreneurial ecosystems. The entrepreneurial ecosystem is a global phenomenon that has attracted the recent interest of scholars (Ratten, 2020 (1&2); Scott et al., 2021; Spigel & Harrison, 2018; Fubah & Moos, 2021). 'Entrepreneurial ecosystems' have been defined differently by scholars, implying the lack of consensus on its definition. Some scholars (Stam & van de Ven, 2021; Isenberg, 2010) have proposed that entrepreneurial ecosystems are composed of different elements, including networks, infrastructure, culture, and intermediaries. All these elements merge with each other to bring about entrepreneurial activities within a set geographical setting.

Research on the significant impact on SMEs during the pandemic has generally been from the West (Kuckertz & Brandle, 2021; Syriopoulos, 2020; Rashid & Ratten,

2021; Ratten (3), 2020; Ratten (4), 2020). When it comes to developing countries like South Africa, which has received very little or no attention in any regard. This is irrespective of the fact that South Africa currently is amongst the most affected countries in the world. Apart from the scarcity of research around COVID-19 in the developing world context, practically nothing much has been done to help these entrepreneurs or SMEs. More specifically, there is lack of research in South Africa which could highlight the struggle around losing jobs, high rate of unemployment and the issues surrounding them that has cropped up. Relying only on government is not a viable option either as economies globally are not much stable. This illustrates there is a gap in research on COVID-19, which are pivotal as they could provide a critical understanding into the impact of the crisis (COVID-19) on entrepreneurship. South Africa, previously has been a hub to the clothing and textile industry and currently is predominant in retail. There are a lot of unemployed population with such skills due to the closure or retrenchment of manufacturing units due to various reasons. Through this case study the authors want to highlight the need for entrepreneurship predominantly in the field of clothing and textiles and bring in the need for everyone to try and help the unemployed and the needy (with skills) within the resources available, especially through the use of simple e-learning platforms or modalities. Although there are many educational courses, programs and short courses available, they vary in their modalities and often cost or geographic location becomes an issue for entrepreneurs to attend and get benefitted from them. At times, the rural communities might have very little knowledge or access to such opportunities due to lack of awareness, hence the low tech, easy access e-learning mode was created to reach out to them.

As discussed earlier, COVID-19 came with its own perks and one of them being wider access to technology and gadgets. Owning gadgets or cellphones is no more seen as a want but a need with all basic app access and not just for emergencies. This gives them the ability to access information from their home. This might help and assist them in generating new and creative ideas and working independently to generate some source of income. Various reviews have supported the fact that web-based interventions result in more engagement for the viewers and generates interest to learn new things.

We created a google sites website, an e-learning intervention to help educate stakeholders by giving them ideas and provide quick innovative ways to make products out of waste (off cuts, fabric swatches as hand downs) as shown in the image below.

Link to the google sites page:
https://sites.google.com/view/makingworthoutofwaste/home

Screenshot from 'Making worth out of waste' home page

We visited the organization "Bambanani for Social Development" in the rural areas of Nyanga township, Cape Town, where we met a team of women who were skilled in sewing. We showed them our students' products and asked them their preferences. They were amazed to see the work and especially the concept of waste management and that these products were made from zero material cost. What also caught their attention was the way student created braids, they used different pockets for patch work, with functionality. On discussion with the head of the Bambanani for Social Development community, we came to know that they intend to train stakeholders from the community who need financial support or to those who have skills and are currently unemployed. To address to their needs, we invited few of these community ladies for few hours and showed them how little things like fabrics of different nature can be put together, how fabrics can be hand braided to give it a trendy look and ended up designing a handbag made of fabrics.

We had in the meantime given the final year clothing and textile engineering students a project where they needed to first come up with ideas on how to make products out of waste i.e., offcuts and fabric swatches which were handed down by manufacturing and retail companies (at no cost). They initially did market research to understand the need of the market and knowledge around products made sustainably to save the environment, then create questionnaire surveys, and get them filled up by stakeholders from their community. Based on these feedbacks, they then got their ideas and made products. This was to prepare them as future entrepreneurs enabling them to make products with zero cost involved when it comes to sourcing raw materials at a time of crisis. The students nailed it by preparing such products which we uploaded on the website as well as on social media platforms to get some feedback and general preferences from possible consumers. Students drew up business plans to pitch them to us lecturers showcasing their understanding of the concept and that their ability to fully run a business. They were informed of the purpose of this project was to assist the skilled yet unemployed mass from our industry and possible stakeholders who run small enterprises by appointing people from the community to help them earn a source of income as well as empower them with the idea to mix and match different off cut fabrics and create beautiful products out of it. This segment of manufacturing products out of waste and leftover fabrics has been seen in South Africa yet it hasn't reached its full potential. Therefore, this could be seen to uplift and support communities in self-sustaining themselves at a time of crisis.

The screenshot below shows few of the examples of the products that were made by our students early this year and have been uploaded on the website for use by anyone from the community. As can be seen from the images, the product involves putting together different type and color of fabrics to give it a meaningful outcome. Not only this there has been a breakdown of small operations that has been put together on the website for the entrepreneurs or anyone to view and learn whenever necessary.

Screenshot from the 'Student project' section

Since South Africa is a developing country, there are many constraints that has always been around, and the pandemic has only added to it, be it connectivity, network issues, loadshedding, strikes, and the like. It affects normal livelihood in many ways the worst one being financial constraints. We have therefore ensured that the images loaded on the website are of low-tech data consuming files and that they are available in various regional languages other than English like – Xitsonga, Zulu, IsiXhosa and Afrikaans. It caters to all the different dialect speaking people of the rainbow nation (South Africa). The students have through their videos tried to explain the reason behind minimizing waste and the need to buy less, be more environmentally friendly by adopting sustainable approaches addressing towards circular economy.

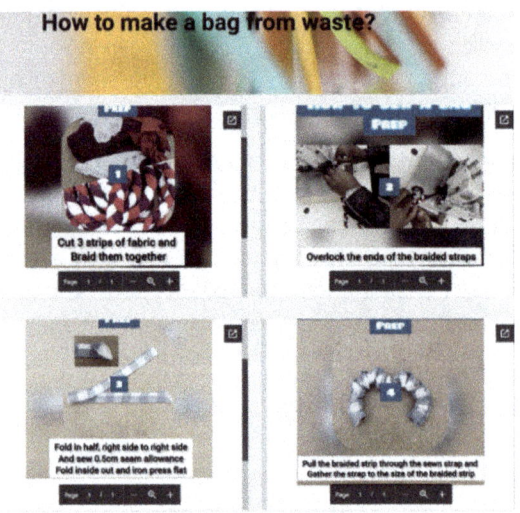

Screenshot from 'Making worth out of waste' processes page

The infrastructure

Dr Sweta Patnaik and Mr Shamil Issacs are the co-creators of this project. Mr Shamil Isaacs is the Manager of Technology Station Clothing and Textiles, CPUT, Cape Town. He is an expert in providing support to the clothing and textile industry to improve innovation and competitiveness in the sector. He has extensive experience in this sector, like, design, innovation, product performance, entrepreneurship and understanding the consumer needs. Through his team he imparts support through workshops, short courses and other similar custom made interventions. Dr Sweta Patnaik is a senior lecturer in the Department of Clothing and Textile Technology, Faculty of Engineering and the Built Environment, where she experts in her teaching approaches, uses e-learning through her teaching, learning and research purposes. She is passionate about her work and working with students on such e-learning interventions, digital storytelling being one of them. She has won few teaching excellence awards for her contribution towards e-learning at the institution level. Other additional members are our students, staff in the lab and the community especially people from the Bambanani for Social Development organisation (their team leader and the ladies who work there).

We thought of coming up with this project with many perspectives in mind. Firstly, the idea was to create awareness among students especially on sustainable approaches, being environmentally conscious, serving back to the community and minimising waste. Then seeing the ideas taking fruition while our students started working on their products gave us a thought if we could take this concept back to the community and see if it could help them in any way seeing the amount of unemployment people in South Africa were facing. Not just this, we did gather some feedback by posting the images of students work on our department's Instagram page to get an idea of consumer preferences where we a lot of good responses using polls.

The website is free, offers easy to access, and is data savvy. The ideas of different operations are shared through images which is published publicly and easily accessible. There are lab experts available to provide extra support if and when needed. However, if any individual with a sewing background is willing to learn and create such products we are willing to provide them with offcuts and let them create such wonderful products out of leftover raw materials. If they can't reach us for sourcing fabrics there are companies/ manufacturing units who gladly hand down their fabrics to entrepreneurs or community run organisations for support. If one would look up for comparing other similar portals it wouldn't be wrong to say that there isn't any such platform created by experts from the education or the clothing and textile industry in South Africa with easy creative ideas that can be used by anyone to earn a living. All that they would need is a sewing machine with some stitching experience would go a long way. Hence these images uploaded in the website will assist them in creating a environmentally friendly, cost saving and trendy product. There are asynchronous lessons that can be made available through the Technology Station Clothing and Textiles as well as support through WhatsApp (as this has been a simpler and easier mode of communication across all ages). The question that would arise at this stage is who will buy such products? There are many platforms and potential customer who will be willing to buy such products – for example conducting market day within the university and inviting staff and students from across the university (which previously gained a lot of momentum) i.e. the university has more than 30 000 students, sell it to the shop owners selling similar products in the urban markets (e.g. The Shed at the Cape

Town Victoria & Alfred (V&A) Waterfront), on the informal markets (flea markets) or exchange amongst each other to meet their requirements.

Other than the images, the videos have narrations which stakeholders can choose to listen in the language of their choice. Through the contact us section they can reach us and express their needs which we will try and cater to by appointing the right staff. The work done by students have been shared as examples for them to use to re-create the design or look of the product based on their preferences. There is a google form link that anyone interested can fill up and reach us directly for support and assistance.

Each product type follows with a set of images with short explanations on how to create that product. There is a section where people visiting the website can contact us by filling in the google form and the same applies if they want to provide feedback to us in terms of changes or suggestions. They can raise their concerns about the webpage and inform us, things that they feel has not been updated to enhance their learner knowledge or want us to include. The webpage follows Clark and Meyer's multimedia principle and best practices to e-learning. This principle allows that stakeholders get to learn better and deeper from words and images (graphics) than words alone and we through our website are using graphics, words and and video clip narration to communicate through the content (Clark and Mayer, 2016). The different breakdown of information via multimedia are designed so that words and images are used to the best of their ability, which is in alignment with the Multimedia principle. The videos, narration and words per slide are generally very less and consume less than 1 mb of data space. Clark and Mayer have recognised that stakeholders master and absorb more deeper through multimedia than when learners experience more social presence, they find it relatable. The content has been divided into sections and each section could viewed and reviewed again. In addition to this, during the design and building up of this website, a sequential, participatory instructional design and development method was carried out. This was carried out using an extensive involvement of stakeholders from the community, staff, students and peers from the industry and from following other similar experts globally through platforms like LinkedIn. There were several phases of development and evaluations that were considered during building this website up:

- Expert suggestions and feedback for each section was carefully done. Various community experts were selected and shown the products initially and feedback was taken. There was feedback taken from probable consumers through social media platforms that showed their preference for buying such products made from waste.

- The ladies from the community with some sewing background were invited to the department to learn, view and understand the process. They were exposed to such creative ideas, how products were put together? and what does the final product look like? They found the information extremely helpful, trendy and creative. They found this learning easy, quick and anywhere anytime access. The design and colour of the background screens, words used and images were appealing to them.
- Through the website we created evaluation and feedback forms and we had few responses where we got some feedback on what stakeholders felt the website contributed towards their learning. Additionally, there were some good responses in terms of effectiveness and quality of learning the website provided. There were a lot of positives about the site and there were some areas of development as well.

To make the process simple and easy there isn't any complexities in terms of technologies. If in case, the website is handed over to other department colleagues at a later stage due to various reasons the hand over will be smooth and easy. Google analytics will be used for web analytics. The videos are constantly created from time to time keeping new trends in mind, and initially images are uploaded followed by series of events explaining the process to make a certain product.

The challenges

There were few challenges that were experienced at an early stage.

- We were unsure how the entrepreneurs and SMEs would see it and what their preferences will be.
- We were also unconfident if the students would come up to some good creative products and it would be easy to learn for the community.
- Another challenge was also if we make the content freely available, in multilingual languages and multimedia e-learning content for entrepreneurs and SMEs. Because the target audience involves people with very little educational background, hence it was important to keep that in mind while developing the website using simple English language.
- We tried not to have too much complexity in the mode of operation and content.
- Promoting this website could also be a challenge in reaching out nationally to all needy entrepreneurs and SMEs although we have spread the word through students, staff and through various social media platforms.

How the initiative was received by the users or participants

The initiative to minimise waste is not new, it has been adopted by various companies, organisations, small businesses in many ways in South Africa and globally. Retailers are coming up with such concepts and ways to bring sustainable waste management into their organisation. They are sending their staff for new and advanced qualifications in order to keep them updated in line with the new approaches and frameworks that the industry should be aware of. However, not much effort has been made to reach out to people especially during pandemic due to various health and safety reasons. When the inflation and fuel prices are skyrocketing managing to run a family is difficult, therefore having members in the family who can still work from home and earn a living will benefit them. The idea took its shape and was completed in November 2019, where students were asked to make similar products and we hosted a market day to spread its awareness and reach out to the community. The work was presented at an international conference in Pretoria. However, early 2020 with the onset of the pandemic it was difficult to take it further, similar were the scenario in 2021. Therefore we tried to bring it back in full form this year and it seemed doable, hence we started by reaching out to entrepreneurs and sharing our ideas and our students work through videos and images. At this stage we have no external funding necessary, therefore we never felt the need to source funding from external sources. This initiative on being shared with the students and staff was very well welcomed and on sharing it with the community we were amazed to see that even the skilled workers liked and appreciated the concept and ideas. They said, they could use these ideas and create products to add to an extra income. Although the feedbacks were more vocal there were few comments which we received via the feedback form from them as follows:

What was your reaction after going through our page?
15 responses

It seems interesting

Excellent

Something that I haven't seen before

Why aren't there more sites like this

Excellent way to present technical aspects to the common public

It's some what very inspirational in the sence of doing something with the waste and just not leaving it there

Exciting to see yhr page with all the different categories. Really was a sight to see

Love the great initiative

What was your reaction after going through our page?
15 responses

It seems interesting

Excellent

Something that I haven't seen before

Why aren't there more sites like this

Excellent way to present technical aspects to the common public

it's some what very inspirational in the sence of doing something with the waste and just not leaving it there

Exciting to see yhr page with all the different categories. Really was a sight to see

Love the great initiative

Lastly, any suggestions or feedback for changes or improvements in order to make learning better.
15 responses

Short videos and picture are easy to learn from

Easy accessible website that can be linked from any post viewed

Frequently create content

And more interesting interactive actions

Well done and excellent work. Perhaps add more products next time.

to implement more people to fix the waste problem so there can make this world a better place

From this qualitative study we could receive widespread interest in our webpage. Quite a few stakeholders appreciated and showed willingness in learning more and more. They felt the processes were simple which could be easily learnt and made by anyone willing to learn and earn a source of income.

The learning outcomes

The process resulted in reflective learning and knowledge creation. Being in its early stage we expect the webpage to attract more stakeholders while we keep it updating it simultaneously. There is knowledge creation in both ways, between information users and providers i.e. students are learning through the projects while at the same time the created content is used to teach and assist in building knowledge for a stakeholder. The google sites platform is proving accessible to all within the reach of their fingertips to learn and support themselves.

Plans to further develop the initiative

The initiative will generate interest among students to come up with similar concepts and ideas that could be shared with the community. An annual competition will be held for community-based entrepreneurs and students and linking this to established business as part of their Corporate social Responsibility. On being accepted broadly the idea is to generate funds through the institution or external funders to create a more professional paid website, currently looking at the demographics of stakeholders this platform suits best. The wish is to have this platform self-sustaining in about 3 years. We intend to research more on this and share this work at national and international platforms. The department seeing the slow yet constant progress along with the Technology Station intends to create what we could call as 'The Entrepreneurial Hub' where a lab-based unit (incubators) could be created where we could provide a platform for the unemployed, alumni from the department who have lost their job or are now willing to be an entrepreneur due to the new world of sustainability and waste management booming in. To also support graduate technotrepreneurs at a high-level using science and engineering to develop new uses or products from waste textiles. We intend to share this initiative with other universities in South Africa offering similar qualifications and work together to help communities. The idea is to establish a community or network of sustainably aware small businesses starting at the university and spreading to the rest of the country linked by an app. Seeing the need and interest in stakeholders, the platform can surely prove effective, efficient and a cost-effective method to address to such educational needs of the community.

References

Kuckertz, A.; Brändle, L. Creative reconstruction: A structured literature review of the early empirical research on the COVID-19 crisis and entrepreneurship. *Manag. Rev. Quart* 2021, 1–27.

Syriopoulos, K. The impact of COVID-19 on entrepreneurship and SMEs. *J. Int. Acad. C. Stud* 2020, *26*, 1–2.

Gregurec, I.; Tomičić Furjan, M.; Tomičić-Pupek, K. The impact of COVID-19 on sustainable business models in SMEs. *Sustainability* 2021, *13*, 1098.

Cancherini, L.; Lydon, J.; Silva, J.S.d.; Zemp, A. What's Ahead for Biotech: Another Wave or Low Tide? McKinsey & Company: 2021. Available online: https://www.mckinsey.com/industries/pharmaceuticals-and-medical-products/our-insights/whats-ahead-for-biotech-another-wave-or-low-tide.

Alessa, A.A.; Alotaibie, T.M.; Elmoez, Z.; Alhamad, H.E. Impact of COVID-19 on entrepreneurship and consumer behaviour: A case study in Saudi Arabia. *J. Asian Financ. Econ. Bus.* 2021, *8*, 201–210.

Ratten, V. Entrepreneurial ecosystems: Future research trends. *Thun. Int. Bus. Rev.* 2020, *62*, 623–628.

Ratten, V. Entrepreneurial ecosystems. *Thun. Int. Bus. Rev.* 2020, *62*, 447–455.

Scott, S.; Hughes, M.; Ribeiro-Soriano, D. Towards a network-based view of effective entrepreneurial ecosystems. *Rev. Manag. Sci.* 2021, 1–31.

Spigel, B.; Harrison, R. Toward a process theory of entrepreneurial ecosystems. *Stra. Entre. J.* 2018, *12*, 151–168.

Fubah, C.N.; Moos, M. Relevant theories in entrepreneurial ecosystems research: An overview. *Acad. Entre. J.* 2021, *27*, 1–18.

Stam, E.; van de Ven, A. Entrepreneurial ecosystem elements. *Small Bus. Econ.* 2021, *56*, 1–24.

Isenberg, D.J. How to start an entrepreneurial revolution. *Harv. Bus. Rev.* 2010, *88*, 40–50.

Rashid, S.; Ratten, V. Entrepreneurial ecosystems during COVID-19: The survival of small businesses using dynamic capabilities. *World J. Entrep. Manag. Sustain. Dev.* 2021, *17*, 457–476.

Ratten, V. Coronavirus (covid-19) and entrepreneurship: Changing life and work landscape. *J. Small Bus. Entrep.* 2020, *32*, 503–516.

Ratten, V. Coronavirus and international business: An entrepreneurial ecosystem perspective. *Thun. Int. Bus. Rev.* 2020, *62*, 629–634.

Clark, R. C. and Mayer, R. E. (2016) *E-learning and the science of instruction*. 4th edn. Wiley.

Author Biographies

Dr Sweta Patnaik is a Senior Lecturer, Teaching & Learning coordinator and Curriculum Officer in the Department of Clothing and Textile Technology, Faculty of Engineering and the Built Environment. Her research interests are around waste management, sustainability, e-learning and blended learning which she publishes nationally and internationally. She has won the Nelson Mandela University Alumni Rising Star Award 2020 as well as the first recipient of the prestigious DAAD UNILEAD scholarship 2021

Mr Shamil Isaacs is the Manager: Technology Station: Clothing and Textiles (Technology Transfer for Clothing and Textiles Small Businesses). He has been part of Department of Science and Technology initiative to support SMMEs in clothing, textile and related sectors throughout South Africa.

The Data-Free Moya Messenger Application: Online Accounting Tutoring in a Large Class

Fazlyn Petersen and Ronald Arendse
University of the Western Cape, Cape Town, South Africa
Fapetersen@uwc.ac.za, Rarendse@uwc.ac.za

Abstract: There is an increased need for more accessible technological options for students, especially during the Covid-19 pandemic. The literature indicates a prevalent digital divide due to the exclusion of students based on their socioeconomic status and their ability to access the internet. Student inclusion can be aided using applications that do not use data (data-free). The South African mobile instant messenger, the Moya Messenger application, is data-free. Using ethnographic research, the Moya Messenger application was piloted in a large accounting class of 495 undergraduate students and 15 tutors during the Covid-19 pandemic. It allowed the lecturer to set up groups for students and tutors to facilitate online tutoring. The Moya Messenger application allowed students to engage with peers and tutors, data-free. The research used the framework for the extraction of lessons learned as a theoretical model. Tutors' feedback was analysed using thematic content analysis. Students' feedback from the course evaluation was analysed using descriptive statistics. The findings for implementing this alternative to the popular WhatsApp option showed positive outcomes. The positive outcomes were due to students having access to tutors, even without data. Most students (79,47%) indicated that the tutor was available and helpful. Tutors indicated that the use of voice notes assisted students in understanding course concepts. Students agreed or strongly agreed (70,2%) that the course allowed them to fully participate. However, at the time of implementation, the application was not yet available to students who used Apple devices. Recommendations for implementing this application in other large classes are to provide a training guide to students. The implementation of the Moya Messenger application will aid students' learning more if the sending of attachments also did not require data.

Introduction

"No student should be left behind. Students who have no study gadgets or internet connectivity should not be treated as though they are the cause of #Covid_19. We will ensure that we take all students along"

The South African Deputy Higher Education Minister, Buti Manamela (Khumalo, 2020).

The need for "inclusive and equitable quality education and promote lifelong learning opportunities for all" is highlighted by the fourth Sustainable Development Goal (SDG) (United Nations, 2017). During the Covid-19 pandemic, there is a need for more accessible technological options for students. Target 4.5 in the fourth SDG supports the elimination of all discrimination in education (UNESCO, 2016), however, there is a prevalent digital divide in South Africa (Statistics South Africa, 2018). The digital divide excludes students based on their socioeconomic status and their ability to access the internet (Cinnamon, 2020).

Access to the internet and devices are important considerations when emergency remote learning was implemented during Covid at tertiary institutions, as indicated by the South African Deputy Higher Education Minister. Despite the growing penetration of mobile phones in South Africa, the number of households with internet access remains low (10.1%) (Statistics South Africa, 2018). The statistics also indicate that 86.9% of South African households used mobile phones exclusively and therefore the cost of data needs to be reviewed (Statistics South Africa, 2018). Mobile companies such as MTN and Vodacom operate in several African countries. The average cost of 1 gigabyte (GB) of Vodacom data in South Africa is higher ($7.83) than in other African countries, such as Mozambique ($2.19) (Healing, 2019).

Mobile operators have zero-rated institutional electronic learning management systems (eLMS) during Covid as part of the State of Emergency being declared in South Africa (Department of Communications and Digital Technologies, 2020). Zero-rating means that students do not need data to access educational resources. The cost of zero-rating is borne by the mobile operators. The University of the Western Cape uses iKamva, an eLMS built on the Sakai platform (University of the Western Cape, 2020). iKamva allows students to engage in synchronous and asynchronous learning (CEICT, 2019). Synchronous learning allows students to engage in real-time, however, it is more data-intensive. Using the BigBlueButton on iKamva for video conferencing is an example of synchronous learning, however, this functionality is currently not zero-rated. Asynchronous learning is not in real-time and is less data intensive. iKamva functionality such as discussion forums are forms of asynchronous learning. Students can use this functionality at a convenient time, but the feedback or responses is not immediate (CEICT, 2019). Discussion forums are zero-rated and more inclusive as students without data will still be able to access them.

It must be highlighted that the current zero-rating of institutional learning management systems, will not remain indefinitely, especially as the State of Emergency was lifted in South Africa on 5 April 2022 (South African Government,

2022). Mobile operators will no longer be compelled to provide access to institutions' eLMS at their cost.

Infrastructure

The research used the framework for the extraction of lessons learned as a theoretical model, as indicated in Figure 1 (Balie & Immink, 2009).

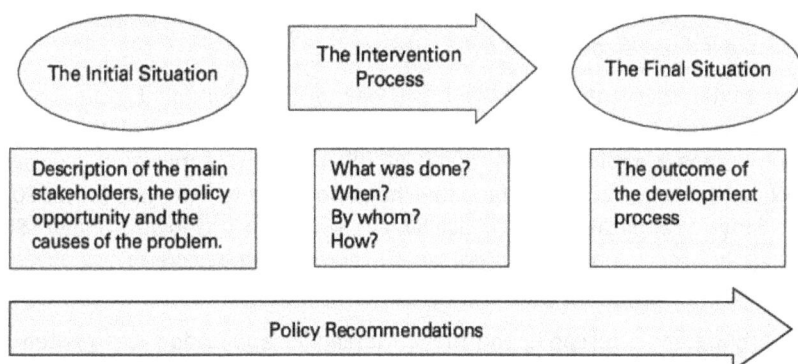

Figure 5: The framework for the extraction of lessons learned (Source: Balie & Immink, 2009)

In the initial situation, tertiary institutions, especially those whose students are predominantly of lower socioeconomic status, needed to consider providing students with more accessible technological options for students, especially during the Covid-19 pandemic. When lockdown commenced, the rapid move to remote learning highlighted existing inequalities (Czerniewicz et al., 2020). The need to engage students via synchronous learning became evident, in the absence of face-to-face engagement.

The primary objective was to provide some synchronous communication with students so that learning could continue online. The initial interventions included the use of existing platforms, such as iKamva. The University of the Western Cape's eLMS was not zero-rated at the commencement of level five lockdown. The lack of zero-rating meant that students may not have received the necessary communication and resources due to a lack of either network, data, or devices. The Accounting lecturer initially created WhatsApp groups with students and tutors, however, this was also limited to students who had data.

Students without data were excluded and as a result, a data-free MIM option was tested among lecturers in the Accounting and Information Systems department. Data-free it "means no data is taken from your airtime or data bundle balance. To use data-free apps you need to keep your mobile data turned on. As long as you are on a partnered mobile network operator such as Vodacom or MTN in South Africa, data-free applications will not use any of your airtime or data balance. However, other applications on mobile phones may use some data. The results of testing the data-free Moya Messenger application were promising. Ten tests were performed to determine the accessibility and usability Moya Messenger application (Petersen, 2020). Ninety per cent of the tests conducted, such as testing for access, were achieved (Petersen, 2020).

As part of the intervention process, it was envisaged that student inclusion could be aided using a data-free application such as the South African MIM, the data-free Moya Messenger application (Petersen, 2020). The Moya application is designed by biNu and has a similar interface to WhatsApp (refer to Figure 2) (biNu, 2020). The Moya application is available via the Google Play Store https://play.google.com/store/apps/details?id=nu.bi.moya&referrer=utm_source%3Ddatafree%26utm_medium%3Dwebsite.

Using ethnographic research, the Moya Messenger application was piloted in a large first-year accounting class of 495 undergraduate students and 15 tutors at the commencement of the Covid-19 pandemic. The application allows data-free messaging and voice notes to be sent. It also allows groups to be created (biNu, 2020). The creation of groups, by the accounting lecturer, allows tutors and lecturers to engage with students even if they do not have data.

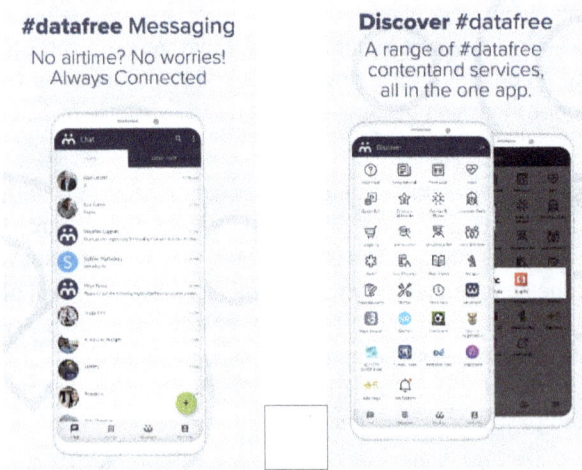

Figure 6: Moya data-free application interface

The data collection was completed at the end of the 2021 academic year and used purposive sampling. Qualitative data was collected from the lecturer via a reflective exercise and the tutors via an online survey and discussions, given Covid-19 restrictions. Students' quantitative feedback was obtained from the course evaluation. The course evaluation was created using Google Forms with a 5-point Likert scale (strongly disagree to strongly agree). The sample size was 151 students, representing a 30.5% response rate. The course evaluation results analysed the students' evaluation of using the Moya MIM. The course evaluation results were analysed using descriptive statistics.

Part of the intervention process included onboarding tutors. The accounting lecturer held a meeting with the tutors via Google Meets. The lecturer explained the need to connect with the unconnected students by using the Moya MIM. Tutors' buy-in was obtained as they confirmed that some students were not joining the WhatsApp tutorials due to data issues. An agreement was reached to use Moya MIM as an alternative, data-free solution to WhatsApp. Students would therefore still be able to obtain important and urgent messages even without data. Students would also be able to connect with tutors and peers.

The first semester was a survival process and anything additional, such as using a new MIM, seemed to overwhelm first-year students. Lecturers and tutors continued using iKamva and WhatsApp. Moya MIM was downloaded by the lecturer and tutors, although it was not available to tutors who were using Apple devices. It must be highlighted that downloading the Moya MIM still requires 15.8 MB of data (biNu, 2020). The first step was to create groups with tutors and students. Students were added using their names and cell phone numbers, collected by the lecturer before lockdown. In the initial implementation, the Moya MIM focused primarily on engaging students who were not responding via WhatsApp.

In the second semester, it was decided to implement the Moya app to use as part of the tutorial programme instead of WhatsApp again. UWC students were still dealing with data, network, and device issues at this point, however, this was not unique to UWC. The lecturer and tutors reinstalled the Moya MIM to have all the tutors and lecturers using the MIM. Groups of students were allocated to tutors and groups were created for each tutor. The links with instructions on how to join tutor groups were sent via email.

The aim of using the Moya MIM was to conduct tutorials via Moya instead of WhatsApp. Students were divided into groups of 25 – 30. Each tutor was assigned one group to conduct online tutorials. During online tutorial groups, students and tutors would work through a tutorial question on a Thursday morning for an hour, via chats, voice notes, images and videos. The creation of groups posed some challenges that will be highlighted in the proceeding section.

The challenges

During the intervention process, challenges became evident. First-year students were not familiar with the eLMS nor learning completely online. To avoid overwhelming first-year students a phased-in approach was implemented with limited technology use.

A tutor also indicated that they had trouble switching to tutoring exclusively online as they preferred tutoring face-to-face. Tutors struggled to download and become familiar with the MIM functionality initially. Three of the fifteen tutors used Apple phones and therefore could not download the Android MIM from the Google Play Store.

Issues were experienced when trying to create groups and have an administrator assigned. When several students tried joining the groups simultaneously, it caused the groups to become unresponsive. The issues were resolved by tutors sending the links to smaller groups daily. The process took a week to complete but limited the number of students joining concurrently.

The use of the Moya MIM required WiFi or mobile data to be switched on, although users are not charged for data used for text messages or voice notes when using the application. Despite the Moya MIM being data-free it still required network access; however, this is limited in more rural South African areas. Sending chats and voice notes were data-free but sending attachments and video was not (biNu, 2020). Students were notified of the size of the attachments and could decide whether they wanted to download them.

How the initiative was received by tutors and students

As per the research model, the final situation allowed the outcome of the implementation to be assessed. Tutors were eager to engage with the students and adapted quickly to using the Moya MIM instead of WhatsApp for online tutoring. The quick adaption was expected as tutors were senior students and were comfortable using technology and devices, unlike the first-year students.

Tutors indicated that it was easier to use the Moya MIM when they were familiar with the course content. Using Moya MIM functionality allowed tutors to use voice notes and pictures to explain the content. The use of pictures allowed tutors to show students how to perform calculations, however, sending pictures was not zero-rated. The finding is supported by.83,44% of students who indicated that the tutor was effective and displayed good knowledge of the materials taught in the course evaluation (refer to Table 1).

Table 2 Tutor effectiveness

	The tutor was effective and displayed good knowledge of taught material
Strongly disagree	2,65%
Disagree	1,99%
Neutral	11,92%
Agree	41,06%
Strongly agree	42,38%
Grand Total	100,00%

Tutors indicated the benefit of using Moya MIM, *"Students could go over the work afterwards as the messages are still there as opposed to face-to-face classes"*. Based on the results from Table 2, students (78,81%) indicated that tutors provided prompt feedback and results.

Table 3 Tutor providing feedback and results

	The tutor provided prompt feedback and results
Strongly disagree	3,31%
Disagree	1,32%
Neutral	16,56%
Agree	35,10%
Strongly agree	43,71%
Grand Total	100,00%

Using the MIM allows tutors to have more flexibility, including scheduling (Pimmer, Lee & Mwaikambo, 2018). A tutor's commitment and flexibility as indicated by the following quote, *"I made myself available outside of the prescribed tutoring times as well as consultation hours to be there for the students with whatever questions they might have"*.

The finding is supported by the results in Table 3. Most students (79,47%) indicated that the tutor was available and helpful in the course evaluation.

Table 4 Tutor availability and helpfulness

	The tutor was available and helpful
Strongly disagree	1,99%
Disagree	3,97%
Neutral	14,57%
Agree	35,10%
Strongly agree	44,37%
Grand Total	100,00%

The learning outcomes

The course evaluation and tutor survey were used to evaluate the achievement of learning outcomes. Based on Table 4, students (76,16%) indicated that there were clear learning objectives.

Table 5: Clarity of learning objectives

	Learning objectives were clear
Strongly disagree	2,65%
Disagree	1,99%
Neutral	19,21%
Agree	55,63%
Strongly agree	20,53%
Grand Total	100,00%

Using Moya MIM increased student participation in online tutoring. The following comment reflects how tutors assessed participation, *"I was able to see who is online, who participates and who views the messages but [also who] does not participate"*. Table 5 supports the tutors' feedback as 70,2% of students agreed or strongly agreed that the course allowed students to fully participate.

Table 6: Course organised to allow all students to participate fully

	Course organised to allow all students to participate fully
Strongly disagree	3,31%
Disagree	4,64%
Neutral	21,85%

Agree	45,70%
Strongly agree	24,50%
Grand Total	100,00%

However, some tutor groups did not participate, *"Most of my students did not make use of the intervention"*. Some students' lack of participation is unexpected as they may not have had devices, or network access or did not want to participate.

The use of Moya MIM to achieve more inclusivity was summarised by a tutor with the following quote: *"I could easily explain the course content and make sure that no student was left behind."*

The literature indicates that there is a positive correlation between online tutoring and student performance (Carlana & La Ferrara, 2021), although this was not measured as part of this research project.

Plans to further develop the initiative

The next phase of this research is to implement the Moya application in more classes across the University of the Western Cape. A large class of third-year Information Systems students has been identified as the next group. Student perceptions will be analysed in more detail, via a quantitative study and the use of a survey. It may be interesting to see the differences between the first-year and third-year students in different departments. More senior third-year students, majoring in Information Systems, may find the Moya application easier to use.

Recommendations for implementing this application in other large classes are to provide a training guide to students. There is now a Moya MIM version available for students who use Apple devices. This version may make the MIM more inclusive. We would appeal to mobile network operators to also reverse bill the use of attachments for institutions in our aim to provide more inclusive learning options for all students.

References

Balie, J. & Immink, M. 2009. Integrating Food Security and Nutrition Issues in National Policies and Strategies: Learning from Country Experiences. In *Food Security Policy. Insights from Mozambique*. Available: https://www.researchgate.net/publication/299490400_Integrating_Food_Security_and_Nutrition_Issues_in_National_Policies_and_Strategies_Learning_from_Country_Experiences [2022, June 02].

biNu. 2020. *#datafree Moya Messenger App*. Available: https://www.datafree.co/moya-messenger-app [2020, April 24].

Carlana, M. & La Ferrara, E. 2021. Apart but Connected: Online Tutoring and Student Outcomes during the COVID-19 Pandemic. *SSRN Electronic Journal*. DOI: 10.2139/ssrn.3777556.

CEICT. 2019. *EMS: Asynchronous & Synchronous Engagement and Simulations to enhance Learning and Teaching*. Available: https://www.uwc.ac.za/elearning/News/Pages/EMS-Asynchronous--Synchronous-Engagement-and-Simulations-to-enhance-Learning-and-Teaching.aspx [2020, April 26].

Cinnamon, J. 2020. Data inequalities and why they matter for development Data inequalities and why they matter for development. *Information Technology for Development*. 26(2):214–233. DOI: 10.1080/02681102.2019.1650244.

Czerniewicz, L., Agherdien, N., Badenhorst, J., Belluigi, D., Chambers, T., Chili, M., de Villiers, M., Felix, A., et al. 2020. A Wake-Up Call: Equity, Inequality and Covid-19 Emergency Remote Teaching and Learning. *Postdigital Science and Education*. 2(3):946–967. DOI: 10.1007/s42438-020-00187-4.

Department of Communications and Digital Technologies. 2020. Amendment of directions on the risk-adjusted sector issued under regulation 4(10) of the regulations made under section 27(2) of the Disaster Management Act, 2002 (Act no. 57 of 2002). *Government Gazette No. 43351*. 3 June: 3–4. Available: https://www.gov.za/sites/default/files/gcis_document/202006/43411gon651.pdf [2022, June 06].

Healing, J. 2019. How do SA's data prices compare with the rest of Africa? *Eyewitness News*. Available: https://ewn.co.za/2019/12/03/how-do-sa-data-prices-compare-with-the-rest-of-africa [2020, July 08].

Khumalo, K. 2020. Manamela hits out at Wits and Co over online learning. *Sunday World*. 19 April. Available: https://sundayworld.co.za/news/manamela-hits-out-at-wits-and-co-over-online-learning/ [2020, April 21].

Petersen, F. 2020. Towards Student Inclusivity during COVID-19: Testing the #datafree Moya Messenger. *Alternation - Interdisciplinary Journal for the Study of the Arts and Humanities in Southern Africa*. SP32(1):294–331. DOI: 10.29086/2519-5476/2020/sp32a12.

Pimmer, C., Lee, A. & Mwaikambo, L. 2018. Is mobile instant messaging: New knowledge tools in global health? *Knowledge Management and E-Learning*. 10(3):334–349. DOI: 10.34105/j.kmel.2018.10.019.

South African Government. 2022. *COVID-19 / Novel Coronavirus*. Available: https://www.gov.za/Coronavirus [2022, June 06].

Statistics South Africa. 2018. General Household Survey, 2018. *Statistical Release P0318*. (May). Available: http://www.statssa.gov.za/publications/P0318/P03182018.pdf.

UNESCO. 2016. Unpacking Sustainable Development Goal 4 Education 2030. *United Nations Educational, Scientific and Cultural Organization*. 33.

United Nations. 2017. *Education for Sustainable Development Goals: Learning Objectives*.

University of the Western Cape. 2020. *About Sakai Help*. Available: https://ikamva.uwc.ac.za/portal/help/main.

Author Biographies

Dr Fazlyn Petersen is a senior Information Systems lecturer at the University of the Western Cape. Her research foci are Information Communication and Technology for Development (ICT4D) in health and education. Her research focuses on creating more inclusive online environments for students and patients, especially those with lower socioeconomic status.

Mr Ronald Arendse is currently the Project Manager of special projects in the Faculty of Economic and Management Sciences at UWC. He is a lecturer and module co-ordinator in Financial Accounting. Previously he assisted academics in using technology to enhance teaching and learning and the implementation of the University Teaching and Learning strategy

Xbox: The Training Ground: Empowering Support Advocates via Engaging Training

C. Sigmund, K. Kulkarni, S. Nayar
chsigmun@microsoft.com
v-kakulkarni@microsoft.com
v-shnayar@microsoft.com
v-singhabhis@microsoft.com

Introduction

Microsoft is the worldwide leader in consumer gaming, with 100 million customers globally (as of 2021). Customer support is managed by 2.1K Advocates, who respond via email, chat, and phone to a broad range of technical and account issues. Previously, an exhaustive 90-hour onboarding programme empowered Advocates with the skills and knowledge to respond to customer inquiries. The programme included 40+ standalone courses made up of primarily asynchronous content, requiring 15 business days to consume. In response to increasing customer demand for support, stakeholders requested that we improve Advocate time to proficiency (TTP) by reducing new hire training time. Subsequently, the learning team reimagined the training by building a learner journey that is directly aligned with the customer experience; it focuses on the most common troubleshooting scenarios and links the content using a single, unified story. We developed a detailed set of diverse customer personas that enabled Advocates to "step into" the customer experience and practice empathy throughout the programme.

Several themes emerged from the Advocate feedback:

- Story helped Advocates connect directly with content in the context of real-life situations.
- Advocates appreciated the use of "conversations" as a learning method.
- Gameplay videos, images and music connected content and context.
- Activities reinforced information and provided frequent, immediate practice.
- Courses focused on the most critical topics that Advocates needed to know.

Most importantly, the programme reduced training time by more than 40% and improved all three KPIs.

KPI	Description	Improvements
Customer Satisfaction (CSAT) {1...5}	Customer rating given after an interaction	+ 4.8%
Helped Resolve (HR) {0...100%}	Proportion of customers who say their issue has been resolved	+ 8.4%
First Contact Resolution (FCR) {0...100%}	Proportion of customers who say issue was resolved after their *first* Advocate contact	+ 10.2%

This effort qualitatively and quantitatively demonstrates the value of using a unified, story-based approach to create complex trainings.

Microsoft Xbox boasts five gaming consoles, hundreds of apps (games) and subscription-based streaming services. The Microsoft Xbox Advocate team delivers robust services to the global user base for issues related to shipping, payment, returns, refunds, exchanges, and subscriptions. Queries range from the simple ("How do I switch on the device?") to the technical ("Why is my device not connecting to my network?"). Customers can reach out to Xbox support via email, phone, chat, and the online Expert community.

Queries are fielded by approximately 1.1K support Advocates. The team is crucial in helping customers build a trusting relationship with the Xbox ecosystem's products and services. They innovate alongside users and develop emotional connections to turn customers into Xbox Fans. Potential customers can connect with an Advocate even before they purchase a console or service to learn more about the advantages of the Xbox over competing consoles and services. Advocates assist customers by:

- Identifying specific gaming needs and delivering corresponding Xbox value-adds.
- Guiding customers through the various purchase channels and payment methods and providing support for issues with delivery, returns and refunds.
- Setting up the device by guiding them on connections, subscriptions, discounts, upgrades, and parental controls.

The Xbox New Hire Redesign project was a five-month endeavour to prepare Advocates for their roles. This project encompassed initial research and stakeholder interviews, reviews of existing content, design sessions and development, testing, and publication of the programme. "Xbox – The Training Ground", our newly designed New Hire programme, was officially released on September 23, 2021.

The Microsoft Customer Experience Framework (CXF)

Every Advocate–Fan interaction is driven by the Customer Experience Framework (CXF). The framework defines three parameters by which an Advocate needs to guide the Fan in query resolution and served as a foundation from which we built the programme:

- Empower Me: When it comes to issue prevention and resolution, customers want to be able to self-serve. And they want it to be a simple and satisfying experience.
- Help Me: Even with an exceptional self-serve experience in place, customers sometimes still need or just prefer to talk with an Advocate. They want to talk to a Microsoft expert who knows what they're doing and can get it done swiftly.
- Advise Me: This drives customer value by helping them get the most from their products and services and introduces new Microsoft solutions that empower customers to achieve more.

The Microsoft CARE behaviours are at the heart of CXF and form the cornerstone of our relationships with our customers. They indicate that a Microsoft representative will:

- Communicate Effectively
- Take Accountability
- Be Resourceful
- Demonstrate Empathy

These behaviours help Advocates deliver exceptional end-to-end Xbox Fan experiences.

The Business Need

With a globally expanding customer base, the existing Xbox onboarding programme needed an overhaul to address two fundamental concerns:

Ensuring a Quicker Time to Proficiency
Advocates must be familiar with a variety of Xbox offerings, plans and consoles and guide customers with accurate information. While the existing New Hire programme encompassed this spectrum of topics, the journey was 90 hours long and the learners had to traverse multiple e-Learning modules and classroom

sessions. Each course ranged anywhere in length from 60 minutes to 3 hours. The curriculum needed greater focus on key topics to provide the right information while improving the time to proficiency.

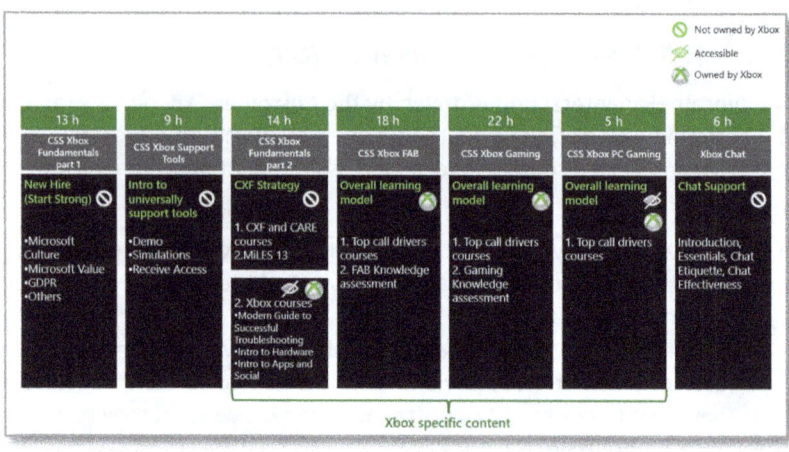

Figure 7: Original Xbox New Hire Programme

Delivering a Role-Based Learning Experience for New Advocates

One challenge with the existing programme was the lack of emotional connection between Advocates and customers. Resolutions to customer issues involved remote troubleshooting with little to no customer involvement. To make the learning experience more authentic, dynamic, and engaging, customers depicted in the training needed plausible backstories. The programme's scenarios needed to be based on the real-life situations of the Fan personas. Finally, it was vital to portray pain points from the Fan's perspective, illustrating what exactly would prompt them to contact the Advocate.

In the new programme, each CARE element is presented through the lens of active customer scenarios with immediate consequences, reinforcing application of the behaviours. Scenario-based training (SBT) of this sort is based on the principles of Situated Learning Theory (Lave & Wenger, 1991), which argues that learning best takes place in the context in which it is going to be used, and situated cognition, the idea that knowledge is best acquired and understood when placed within a related context (Kindley, 2002). Scenario-based training aligns material being taught with situations employees might see in their daily work. Learners find scenario-based training more motivating than traditional instructional formats because solving a work-related problem makes the learning immediately relevant (Lave & Wenger, 1991).

The infrastructure

Creation of the New Hire experience involved a range of expertise; the project was extensive, taking five months to complete. The project was led by a Senior Program Manager (SPM) who represented the business. The SPM oversaw all aspects of design and development with accountability for delivering the final product, managing all project resources, setting and achieving key benchmarks and identifying and resolving barriers to delivering a product that exceeded initial requirements.

Ensuring that design and development activities aligned effectively with the information presented was a critical part of the design effort. Throughout the project, we leaned on the knowledge of experts in our in-house community, including Learning & Development, the Business Program Manager, and the Content Management team. These subject matter experts (SMEs) engaged in weekly reviews to validate that the project addressed the most important learning objectives and that activities were effectively applied.

The content design, development and coding and development work was conducted by a contracted vendor development team at Accenture Services Pvt Ltd, which built the experience using Microsoft Office, Articulate Storyline and Adobe Creative Suite. The development team included experts in graphic design, videography, instructional design, LMS operations and application development.

Pre-Design Workshop

The redesign journey began with a detailed evaluation of the existing training in collaboration with SMEs and trainers. We conducted a weekly workshop to:

- Define the vision for the program.
- Create a consistent story across the experience to link all the content within a common context.
- Provide opportunities for learners to experience issues and resolutions from multiple customer perspectives.
- Create detailed backstories and personas for each customer profile; including the specific challenges they faced and the diverse emotions they might present when contacting Advocates for support.

Programme Design and Key Innovations

A review of the results from the original modules highlighted the need for a new approach to effectively reinforce learning and practical application, engage users, drive participation, and improve knowledge retention. The previous modules were built on a templatised framework and lacked innovation or creativity. As a result, learners were exposed to a repetitive set of visual cues, similar and minimal levels of interactivity and limited practical assessment mechanisms. This resulted in a less interesting and an unengaging experience for the learner. One recognised drawback of using such traditional training methods, particularly in the e-Learning space, is the increased rate of learner abandonment during courses (Gioia, 2016). This becomes especially problematic when learners must complete long or seemingly less relevant curricula, such as the so-called "soft skills" materials often presented to Advocates. This creates a substantial risk of training fatigue, which is directly related to the learners' declining motivation to learn the assigned material, the degree of interactivity incorporated in the training and the production quality of the course (Bennett, 2007). Clearly, identifying ways to train staff that are engaging and more effective at encouraging them to complete training is a critical exercise with potentially substantial impact (Peters, 2019).

Digital Storytelling

The Training Ground employs digital storytelling (DS) to immerse and involve learners in the content. "Digital storytelling is an innovative pedagogical approach that has the potential to engage learners in student-centered learning and enhance learning outcomes across the curriculum" (Smeda et al, 2010). DS uses a common theme or premise throughout a training programme to continually reinforce learning objectives and coherently tie them together. DS methods have been proven to increase learner satisfaction, reduce time to proficiency and improve training abandonment rates. As an example, a prominent U.S. West Coast healthcare system that implemented DS was able to cut its new hire onboarding time by 50% while simultaneously improving retention rates (Sigmund, 2015). Most importantly, storytelling is a fully interactive and immersive approach to learning that encourages learners to "develop their creativity to solve important problems in innovative ways" (Ohler, 2008). In an environment that expects staff to think quickly and resolve complex customer issues, DS is an effective mechanism to train them to be more resourceful and, ultimately, more productive. According to Caine and Caine (1994), if learners' "brains [are filled] with miscellaneous facts and data without any connection, the brain becomes like a catchall closet into which items are tossed and hopelessly lost. But stories help us to organise and remember information and tie content together." Moreover, stories enable learners to form mnemonic devices to connect ideas both within and across chunks of content, increasing short- and long-term knowledge retention. These improvements give learners the ability to synthesise material more effectively into their understanding of their daily activities, draw conclusions about how to apply their knowledge and identify thematic relationships across content.

During the pre-design workshop, we identified the need to incorporate a story to tie in the different experiences of Fans. This, in turn, led us on a journey to create relatable, well-rounded characters who would each have mini spin-off stories that would all come together by the end of the Xbox programme.

The programme is a series of 55 online courses that are linked through a central and joint story, a set of characters and their relationships. Each course deals with a specific topic or set of related topics (purchase, warranties, Xbox services, etc.). As the story unfolds, the lives of the characters are explored further and the connections between them are uncovered.

Courses are divided into "Seasons" based on the type of content, story, and personal journey of each character. Opportunities for Advocates to acquire the precise skills they would use when serving Fans are woven into each season of the story. Most significantly, participants are offered hands-on activities throughout the programme in which they practice and demonstrate these skills.

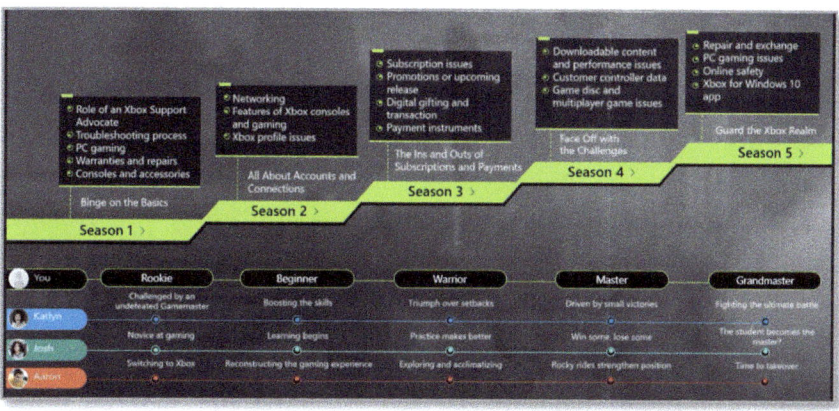

Figure 8: Training Ground Story and Learner Journey

Content

To create the new experience, we first conducted a detailed content analysis of the current courses and extracted the critical information to structure outlines. These outlines served as the foundational material for the overall programme story and design.

Design and Development

The Training Ground presents a robust learning experience in a creative and unique way that leverages high-fidelity graphics, video, and audio to immerse learners in a topic-relevant, Xbox-themed environment.

One priority was to ensure that the model was representative of its users, both visually and in its accessibility, and one way we did this was to include diverse representation for our characters.

Figure 9: Summary of The Training Ground Experience

The challenges

The key challenges stemmed from the need to blend knowledge of the Xbox ecosystem with the softer aspects of customer interaction. One could not be more important than the other. To that end, the need was a story that tied all these aspects together. The story had to:

- Take the learners through the characters' journeys, get them excited and make them want to complete the programme.
- Incorporate core Microsoft Customer Experience Framework values.
- Focus on issues from the customer's perspective.
- Demonstrate the specific obstacles each type of Fan might face and how the Advocate would partner with them to troubleshoot and resolve the obstacle.

Microsoft's mission to empower everyone to achieve more is rooted in empathy-driven interactions with customers. Every conversation depicted in the programme included elements of empathy, such as using collaborative words ("I understand"), referring to the customer by name to establish a connection, and acknowledging the customer's concerns. The conversations also provided Advocates with hints on how to interact with customers of different backgrounds. Based on the customer's familiarity with Xbox offerings, each conversation was customised to deal with the root cause of the customer's concern and empower them to seek help from online Xbox resources should they face similar situations in future.

Focusing on the Customer's Issues

The Xbox New Hire Reimagined programme focused on the client and the issues they face. This added a more human touch to the courses by presenting Xbox issues from the customer's perspective and the difficulties they face when they are unable to do what they love—gaming. Advocates were introduced in courses when the customer's issue was complex or there were no readily available help articles. In such cases, the Advocates' language expressed a genuine desire to remedy their customer's issue and put themselves in their customer's place. Some issues were even resolved by more experienced gamers within the stories created for each course—this approach was intended to reinforce the concepts of self-help and empowering customers with knowledge.

How the initiative was received by the users or participants

From a learner perspective, the programme was a success. The average learner satisfaction score {1...5} across the 55 individual courses was 4.5, with a 98.7% Top Box. When asked about the relevance of the content to their role and their ability to apply the knowledge, they rated the programme 4.5 with a 99.5% Top Box.

Finally, when queried about their confidence with the support content and their ability to assist Fans before and after each of the courses, the average increased by .45 points, a 9.5% increase.

Qualitative Feedback

We also sought feedback from those who completed the new programme. Some common themes emerged:

- The use of a story helped Advocates connect directly with the content and place it in the context of real-life situations.
- Advocates appreciated the use of "conversations" between Fans and Advocates as a teaching method. The scenario felt authentic and helped pace the information, so it didn't feel too "heavy".
- Placing content in the "Xbox world" with game play and game images made it more engaging and interesting and helped connect the design to the story and the information being presented.
- The well-balanced mix of content and "do" activities reinforced information and provided an opportunity to immediately practice what was presented.
- Courses focused on the most important or critical topics that Advocates needed to know and revisited these topics several times.
- The training felt like Xbox!

Here are select participant quotes:

- "The story carries you through the customer's experience and how you are solving problems for them."
- "This was definitely specifically designed for Xbox, and the other courses we had to take were more general and didn't seem connected to what we do."
- "It actually helped me connect with the information and want to learn it better. I was intrigued by the design, and it got me involved in the courses."
- "I am glad they connected the stories to real life and put themselves in our shoes so they understand what we go through and how we have to help our customers."
- The learning outcomes (what was achieved and how the outcomes were measured/evaluated)
-

Quantitative Improvement

Business success of this programme was evaluated through the combination of reduced training time—more than a 40% overall reduction, resulting in a realised cost avoidance of approximately $1.2 million in the first eight months—and improvement on all three business KPIs. Comparing KPIs between Advocates who completed New Hire training in its original form (January 2021) and those who completed the *Xbox – The Training Ground* reimagined programme (December 2021) shows clear evidence of the new programme's success. All three KPIs improved, with CSAT[2] increasing by 4.8%, HR[3] improving by 8.4% and FCR[4] increasing by 10.2% overall.

Applicability to Other Settings and Environments

While this programme was developed to meet the specific needs of a corporate training program, the experience is firmly rooted in the fundamental principles of Project-Based Learning (PBL).

The traditional PBL model consists of seven primary characteristics:

- Emphasis on open-ended, empirically-focused questions
- Blends a combination of knowledge and application from multiple disciplines to resolve a challenge

---

[2] CSAT – A measure of satisfaction on a 5-point scale given by the customer after contact to rate the support received

[3] HR – The proportion of all cases taken by a support advocate that are resolved by that advocate

[4] FCR – The proportion of customer issues / cases that customers indicated were resolved on the first contact with support

- Is inquiry-based, and generates thought-provoking questions as it helps learners evaluate options
- Requires non-technical applications of skills such as critical thinking, communication, collaboration, and creativity to be successful
- Allows for learner choice in the solutioning process
- Provides opportunities for feedback and revision of the plan and the project, just like in real life
- Requires learners to share their thought processes and results to facilitate discussion and advanced problem solving

As the main story was centered around challenges and problems customers face in the real world, it allowed the development team to apply the same PBL principles and framework that a classroom teacher might. As the Buck Institute for Education (BIE) explains, with PBL, students "investigate and respond to an authentic, engaging, and complex problem or challenge" with deep and sustained attention (PowerSchool, 2021). The application of the red-thread story gives learners a focal point for applying the knowledge that they learn. This reinforces for the learner that they have gained the capability to evaluate and break down future challenges problems into their component parts, lead a diverse team of stakeholders to more thoroughly assess the problem, and develop and implement a solution. Instead of short-term memorization and summative regurgitation, when implemented in this way PBL offers an opportunity for students to engage deeply with the content, bringing about a focus on long-term retention. Previous research, including that by Strobel & van Barneveld (2009) and Walker & Leary (2009) demonstrates that PBL increases long-term retention of content, helps students perform as well as or better than traditional learners in high-stakes events, improves problem-solving and collaboration skills, and improves students' attitudes toward learning.

Plans to further develop the initiative
Upskilling

Now that the programme has been launched and we have more detailed feedback from Advocates and trainers, we have identified some areas for continued enhancement. For example, we will be creating additional content for specific topics, such as cloud gaming and networking, to dive even deeper into the technical troubleshooting processes. This content will be incorporated into the programme as "pro tips" that can easily be accessed from within a given course. In this same vein, trainers and SMEs have requested more advanced, ongoing training to continually upskill our Advocates. As a result, we are currently designing six topic-specific mini learning paths (LPs) comprised of five to six microlearning courses, each focused on a single advanced skill. Starting 30 days after the completion of the New Hire programme, Advocates will be served one of these LPs per month. Upon completing all six, they will be identified as having advanced Advocate skills.

Course Refresh

As previously mentioned, using Xbox game elements and design in the aesthetic of each course, including game sounds, game play video and game images, was one aspect of making the new programme more consumable and engaging. Because of the extremely positive response we received from both learners and stakeholders for this design, we are now in the process of "refreshing" 135 previously released courses so that they have a similar look and feel and fit more appropriately within the "Xbox family" of training.

References

Benefits of Scenario Based Training https://www.nttinc.com/blog/scenario-based-training-2/

Bennett, C. (2007). How long should an e-learning course be? eLearn Magazine August 2007. http://elearnmag.acm.org/featured.cfm?aid=1291532

Caine, R., and Caine, G. 1994. Making Connections: Teaching and the Human Brain. Rev. ed. Menlo Park, Calif.: Addison-Wesley

Gioia, J. (2016). *Abandonment in eLearning Courses and How to Avoid it*. Retrieved from https://www.aftermarketnews.com/the-herman-trend-alert-abandonment-in-elearning-courses-and-how-to-avoid-it/

Kindley, R. W. (2002). *Scenario-based e-learning: a step beyond traditional e-learning*. ASTD Magazine. Retrieved from http://www.astd.org/

Lave & Wenger, E. (1991). Situated Learning: Legitimate Peripheral Participation. New York: Cambridge University Press. https://doi.org/10.1017/CBO9780511815355

Smeda, N., Dakich, E. and Sharda, N. (2010). *Developing a framework for advancing e-learning through digital storytelling*. IADIS International Conference e-learning 2010, Ed.

Ohler, J. (2008). Digital storytelling in the classroom: New media pathways to literacy, learning and creativity, Corwin Press, Thousand Oaks, CA.

Peters, J., and Cornetti, M. (2019). Deliberate Fun: A Purposeful Application of Game Mechanics to Learning Experiences, Sententia Gamification, Austin, TX.

"Project-based learning: Benefits, examples, and resources." *PowerSchool*, June 14, 2021. (1) New Messages! (powerschool.com)

Sigmund, C. (2015). *The PeaceHealth Journey* [Unpublished article]. PeaceHealth.

Tucker, C. (2016). *The benefits of scenario-based learning*. Retrieved from https://www.christytuckerlearning.com/benefits-scenario-based-learning/

"What is PBL." *Buck Institute for Education,* 2022. "Doing a Project" vs. Project Based Learning | PBLWorks

Author Biographies

Chuck Sigmund is the learning and development strategy lead for Xbox worldwide. He brings more than 20 years experience to his role, with a particular emphasis on developing gamified and engaging training programs that deliver measurable results. His work is supported by a Masters in Economics with a focus on research and statistics, and a Masters in Adult Education and Training.

Shruti Nayar has over 11 years of experience in the learning and content domains. She's based out of Bangalore and works with the Learning Experience Design and Development (LEDD) team within Accenture Operations. She kickstarted her career in the edtech industry and moved on to digital marketing but soon found herself going back to the corporate L&D field as an Instructional Designer. She is passionate about creative writing, storytelling, and facilitation.

Kapil Kulkarni has been an instructional designer since 2008. Prior to his experience in the training development domain, he was a graphic designer in the advertising industry and specialized in logo design. He has a passion for graphic design, board and video games, and the visual arts. He works with the Learning Experience Design and Development (LEDD) team within Accenture Operations. He is based in Mumbai, India.

Stop Predatory Practices – Teaching module

Tereza Šímová[1], Zychová Kristýna[2] Paulová Kristýna[2]
[1]Institute of Philosophy of the Czech Academy of Sciences, Czech Republic
[2]Czech University of Life Sciences Prague, Czech Republic
simovat@flu.cas.cz
zychovak@lib.czu.cz
paulova@lib.czu.cz

Abstract: Predatory journals, publishers, and conferences are a pressing problem for the academic community. Predatory practices can manifest in poor quality or incredibly fast peer review, imitation of reputable publishers, falsification of editorial boards, constant spamming, the inclusion of false or fabricated citation indicators, and much more. Initiative Stop Predatory Practices aims to raise awareness of predatory practices across the research community. Our initiative had three objectives – to open a discussion about predatory practices in the Czech Republic, to create an open teaching module, and to raise awareness about predatory practices using educational videos on TikTok and Instagram. The initiative targets master's students, Ph.D. students, and junior and senior researchers. In this case study, we describe the motives for the creation of our initiative, the approach we followed in developing the open teaching module, the challenges we faced, and the initiative's plans for the future. We hope that this case study will become an inspiration for anyone planning to create a similar initiative or just an open teaching module.

Introduction
Motivation for creating the Stop Predatory Practices initiative

Predatory journals, publishers, and conferences (further referred to as predators) are a pressing problem threatening the academic community's reputation. In the context of "publish or perish" (Clapham, 2005), are predators topical as some higher education institutions throughout the world view a publication by itself as adequate proof that an academic is doing research (Gerashchenko, 2022). This problem is primarily related to research evaluation and scholarly publishing. Predatory practices can take many forms, including low-quality, rapid or no peer review, hiding information about article processing charges, relentless spamming, faked or fraudulent citation indicators, imitation of reputable publishers, misrepresenting or falsifying editorial boards, violations of copyright or scholarly ethics (Elmore and Weston, 2020; Kratochvíl *et al.*, 2020; Akça and Akbulut, 2021; Mathew, Patel and Low, 2021) and many others which are constantly evolving and improving. As Tsigaris and Teixeira da Silva (2021) point out, using any lists has not proved to be an effective solution, especially concerning that there is just a binary option - predatory or not. Although many different efforts exist to improve the current situation, e.g. Think.Check.Submit (2022), Think.Check.Attend (2022) or project Combatting Predatory Academic Journals and Conferences (Interacademy Partnership, 2022).

In 2013, the European Commission stated that higher education faces a digital challenge (European Commission, 2013). To enhance the digitalization of education is crucial to combine online learning with face-to-face teaching, e.g., through Massive Open Online Courses, which allow individuals to access learning anywhere, anytime, and on any device (European Commission, 2013). The Covid-19 pandemic has further increased the need for online teaching resources. Cahapay (2020) even suggests that it is necessary to include online or blended learning forms in every curriculum after the Covid-19 pandemic.

For those reasons, the initiative Stop Predatory Practices aims to raise awareness of predatory practices across the research community, not only in the Czech Republic but worldwide, through an open teaching module. The initiative targets master's students, Ph.D. students, and junior and senior researchers - in this document, we refer to them all as students.

Objectives of the initiative

Our initiative had a total of three objectives – initiation of discussion, creation of teaching module, and raising awareness about the issue of predatory practices. The individual objectives are described in more detail below.

Initiation of discussion about the issue of predatory practices

The first objective was to initiate a discussion about predatory practices which scientists are facing in the Czech Republic. This goal aimed to spark a discussion and acknowledge that predators are a severe problem for the scientific community. To achieve this objective, we organized a discussion with key representatives of the scientific community. In this discussion, over 50 researchers, librarians, and Ph.D. candidates shared their experiences and challenges in predatory publishing. The information obtained from the discussion was then summarized in a report describing the situation of the Czech scientific community in the investigated area (Šímová, Zychová, and Paulová, 2022b).

Teaching module

The second goal of our initiative was to create a teaching module. The module focuses on acquiring students' knowledge, skills and competencies, e.g., deepening the knowledge of how to recognize a predatory journal, ability to recognize the basic characteristics of the trustworthy conference, and more generic skills such as developing the student's ability to argue and defend their opinion.

In line with UNESCO's (2019) and European Commission's (2013) recommendations for Open Educational Resources, we have created an open teaching module that is licensed under Creative Commons 4.0 (CC-BY-SA) to ensure easy sharing. When creating the teaching module, we combined the information gathered from discussions with key stakeholders, the current state of the art, and our librarian experience. We aim to create a module that will also apply to a person who does not have a deep orientation on the topic. The module is ready for immediate use without additional preparation. Cobb, Watson, and Ellis (2018) suggested that creating online teaching modules expands the range of learning products and increases flexibility in teaching. For that reason, we prepare the teaching module as modular (like Lego), so if the lecturer wants to select only one, two, or more parts, this is easily possible.

The teaching module consists of a presentation, interactive exercises, and instruction for the trainer (methodology for using the module). The presentation cover topics such as an introduction to predatory publishing, publishers, and journals, their characteristics, examples, and how to recognize them. As Beauchamp and Kennewell (2010) suggest, fostering more dialogical and synergistic approaches in group and individual activities in the educational process is beneficial. Thus, the explanatory part is complemented by interactive exercises to expand students' skills and create dialogue and synergy.

The exercises are based on the principle of constructivist pedagogy. The exercises are designed to cover the whole teaching process from the introduction (activation of students) through practical verification of the theoretical part of the presentation to the conclusion (reflection on the newly acquired knowledge). Some exercises are prepared in the form of worksheets for students to work independently (see Figure 1), and others in the form of discussion or reflection. A detailed methodological guide accompanies each exercise on how to implement the exercise into teaching (an example can be seen in Figure 2). Each Methodological guide for the exercise contains the exercise and teaching targets, information about implementation into teaching, exercise parameters, scenario, and possibility for the online version. A detailed description of the activities will help instructors and self-learners to understand the activity correctly.

Travelling without predators	
Task: Find a conference from your scientific field that will be held this year or next year and you would consider its attending. Then examine it and decide if it is credible in your opinion and why. Do not hesitate to use various information resources for getting information about the conference.	
Chosen conference:	
Area to consider	**Notes**
Conference focus	
Membership, metrics, partners	
Conference details	
Information about published proceedings	
Web presentation – form, professionality	
Final evaluation	

Source: Own elaboration – presentation, Šímová, T., Zychová, K. and Paulová, K. (2022a)
Figure 10: Preview of the worksheet " Travelling without predators"

Travelling without predators

Exercise target
Students will verify the credibility of their chosen conference.

Teaching targets of the exercise
1. To deepen the knowledge about predatory conferences.
2. To verify the ability to recognize the basic characteristics of credible conferences.

Exercise type
Practical exercise in groups with use of the internet, consequent discussion of the results. The exercise is focused on the development of the critical thinking of students.

Implementation into teaching
The exercise takes at least **15–20 minutes** and it has a summarizing character, we recommend scheduling it rather in the second part of the training. At first the students should get information on how to evaluate journals according to their quality from the previous interpretation and consequently they should try the evaluation on their own in this exercise.

Exercise parameters
- Number of students
  - Suitable for groups from **9 to cca 25 students**
- Time required
  - **15 minutes** plus for each group cca **3 minutes** extra
- Necessary aids
  - Printed worksheets for students, internet connection (computers are usually not needed, e.g. mobile phones of the students are enough)

Exercise scenario
1. The students will divide into groups of 3 to 5 members.
2. The students will get worksheets. It is also appropriate to show them samples of invitations to suspicious conferences.
3. Task: Find on the internet a conference that will be held this year or next year and you would consider its attending. Then examine it and decide if it is credible in your opinion and why. You have 10 minutes to determine if the conference is credible or not.
4. In each group one speaker will introduce the opinion of his/her group.
5. The tutor will summarize the results and he/she will end the exercise.

Online variant
1. If possible, the students will divide into groups (breakout rooms). If it is not possible, the students can work also each one for himself/herself.
2. The worksheet will be sent to the students with the task assignment. Consequently the students will work either on their own or in groups for 10 minutes.
3. If possible, in each group one speaker will introduce the opinion of his/her group.
4. If the students will work on their own, it is possible to use online voting for the answer (Slido or similar application). Here it is appropriate to let the selected students comment on particular parts.

Source: Own elaboration – presentation, Šímová, T., Zychová, K. and Paulová, K. (2022a)
Figure 11: Example of methodological guide for exercise

For easy use in teaching and self-study, we have created a methodology for implementation in teaching. The module is also ready for self-study (as a form of e-learning). Figure 3 shows a preview of the teaching module, which contains both the pre-prepared slides and the spoken word transcript. The transcript serves as an assistant for the lecturer and for students who want to go through the explanatory part independently.

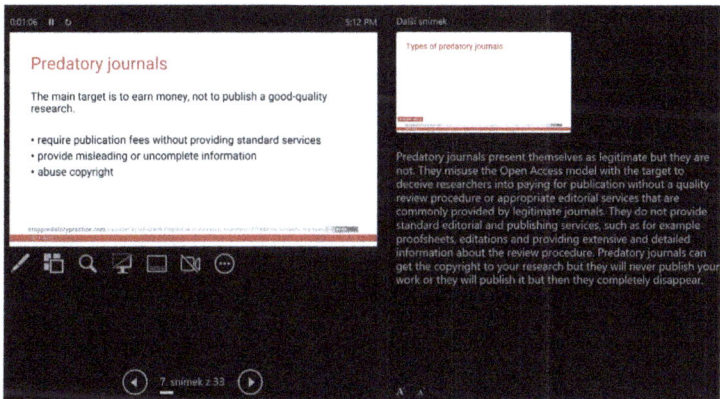

Source: 1 Own elaboration – presentation, Šímová, T., Zychová, K. and Paulová, K. (2022a)

Figure 12: Preview of the teaching module

The teaching module is in Czech and English and is prepared for online and face-to-face teaching. The teaching module is available on the initiative website (Stop Predatory Practices, 2022), where students can also find accompanying resources and other materials to help them fight predatory practices. To ensure the availability of the teaching module and its long time preservation is the teaching module also available at Open Science Framework (Šímová, Zychová and Paulová, 2022a). All materials are available under a Creative Commons 4.0 (CC-BY-SA) license to ensure easy sharing, changes etc.

Raising awareness of the issue of predatory practices

The third objective of the initiative includes popularizing awareness of predatory practices. We are creating videos for TikTok and Instagram, presenting the issue of predatory practices in an interactive and innovative form. As part of these activities, two high school students from the "Otevřená věda" internship are involved in the project. "Otevřená věda" is an internship by the Czech Academy of Sciences, where high school students engage in scientific activities. Involving high school students is not only enriching in terms of introducing them to science but also very enriching in terms of getting the younger generation's perspective on the topic. For popularization, we use elements of storytelling and animated personas (Bitmoji) to represent the issues of predatory publishing – see Figure 4.

Source: Own elaboration based on Bitmoji and social media profiles @open_scientist and @tersi_science.

Figure 13: Examples of bitmoji and posts on social media

Infrastructure

A total of five people created the initiative. Two of them promoted the initiative both at the level of libraries of academies of sciences in the country and at university libraries. The other two members are representatives of university libraries (one focused on library education and the other on open science issues). The last member is a representative of the Czech Academies of Sciences, which also specializes in open science, among other things.

The teaching module is designed to be used with as few equipment requirements (both software and hardware) as possible. The instructor only needs a computer, projector, internet connection, and possibly printing facilities. The basic Microsoft Office package (Word, PowerPoint) will be sufficient for the software. Similar requirements apply to a student who decides to self-study.

Challenges along the way

The challenge was to involve high school students in the project. As this was a voluntary activity and any obligations did not bind them, the collaboration was challenging at some points. For example, one of the students went on Erasmus and completely cut off communication. Nevertheless, the collaboration was exciting and enriching to see a different perspective of high school students who have not yet encountered predators. Overall, making videos has been challenging because TikTok and Instagram do not seem to be the right platform for raising awareness about predatory practices (or at least it has not met the expected response).

How the initiative was received by the participants

Already in the process of developing the teaching module, our initiative has met with a positive response. There is currently no similar initiative in the Czech Republic focusing on the issue of predatory practices. Thanks to the involvement of the project investigators in several associations, research institutions, etc., key stakeholders' participation was relatively easy. We used the networks of the Czech Academy of Sciences, the Library of the Academy of Sciences, university libraries, and members of the Information Education and Information Literacy Working Group (Assoc. of Libraries of Czech Universities) and the Association of Doctoral Students of the Czech Republic. Thus, information about our project reached every research library in the Czech Republic. Junior and senior scientists, publishers' representatives, and Ph.D. students also learned about our initiative.

After we published our teaching module, there was another wave of support from the scientific community. A prominent Czech scientific magazine published an interview with the initiative's founder. We were invited to two Czech librarian conferences, one conference in Florida, USA, and we also presented our results to European Academies' Science Advisory Council members.

During the summer of 2022 we used the teaching module to introduce the issue of predatory practices to librarians and scientific and technical staff of the university. Participants in these sessions especially appreciated the interactive exercises and the clear interpretation of this issue.

The data we currently have available indicates the reach of the Stop Predatory Practices initiative. For example, the Report from the discussion in the Czech Republic currently (September 2022) has over 440 views on Zenodo (Šímová, Zychová and Paulová, 2022b), and almost 1 650 users have visited our website (Stop Predatory Practices, 2022). The short videos we create on social media have been viewed more than 500 times on average. Based on the Open Science Framework data, 26 people have downloaded the teaching module.

We are also collecting feedback on the initiative and the teaching module on the initiative website. We are asking all participants to fill in a short feedback form for us to update and improve our learning module or website. One of the answers, for example, contains a suggestion to extend the teaching module to include the issue of predatory publishing houses: "this is a problem I repeatedly encounter (Czech and foreign publishers who print everything for a fee) and I would like to have some guidelines for these cases. Otherwise, thank you very much for the preparation, I will use it in teaching," says one of the users of the teaching module.

The learning outcomes

"The teaching module covers areas of predatory publishing, publishers, and predatory conferences, it also deals with explaining basic Open Access principles. Primarily it is intended for teaching doctorals, beginning and senior scientists. After minor customizations it can also be used for pre-gradual students" (Šímová, Zychová and Paulová, 2022a). The theoretical part is divided into several areas, such as brief characteristics of open access, an introduction to predatory publishing, and characteristics of predatory journals, and conferences with examples. At the end of the theoretical part, students will learn what to do if they have accidentally published in a predatory journal or conference. The theoretical part aims at gaining theoretical knowledge of predatory publishing. As mentioned above, the theoretical part is complemented by practical exercises focusing on acquiring practical skills that will help students not succumb to predators. After completing the teaching module, students:

- Are able to recognize a predatory journal, publisher, and conference.
- Are able to identify signs of predatory behavior.
- Are aware of the moral principles of publishing.
- Are able to define characteristics of a predatory journal, publisher, and conference.
- Are able to assess the journals' credibility according to the chosen measures.
- Are able to think critically and verify the information.
- Are able to develop the student's ability to argue and defend their opinion.

As this is a relatively new initiative (the teaching module was completed in April 2022), we do not yet have sufficient data for a more comprehensive evaluation. For now, we are only aware of the units of use of our teaching module – as we stated above.

If we look at the learning objectives from a different perspective, from the perspective of the creators of the learning module (librarians and researchers), we can identify additional learning objectives. From the discussion (the first objectives of the initiative) we identified key issues that were certain learning outcomes that served not only as a basis for the creation of the teaching module but also reflect the current situation in the Czech Republic. Among the most pressing issues addressed by researchers in the Czech Republic in the area of predatory publishing are e.g. identification of trusted journals and publishers, shady journals (journals that are not clear predators, however show certain unethical elements), publishing ethics and also research assessment vs. predatory journals (Šímová, Zychová and Paulová, 2022b).

Plans to further develop the initiative

In the winter term we plan to include our teaching module in five courses for Ph.D. candidates at the Czech University of Life Sciences in Prague (approx. 120 students). At the same time, we are preparing free courses for senior and early career researchers, technical staff, and all other interested students at the university mentioned above.

We also plan to use the teaching module across libraries and universities in the Czech Republic in the following months. Moreover, improving our teaching module based on the feedback (as mentioned above). At the same time, we plan to expand our teaching module to include other parts - e.g., more comprehensive and sophisticated Massive Open Online Courses, which will cover predatory publishing and the overall modes of scholarly communication and publishing. Another exciting concept and way to expand our initiative is to create a community of "open access heroes". This topic came out of a discussion about predatory practices in the Czech Republic (Šímová, Zychová and Paulová, 2022b). It is, therefore, possible that our initiative will create medallions about authors who support open access and combat predatory practices and thus create a collection of good practice examples. As before, we want to follow the principles of open educational resources in our future activities as UNESCO (2019) and the European Commission (2013) recommended. We also want to focus more on bachelor's and master's students. We plan to prepare a board game for them, which will introduce them to the issue of predatory publishing in an interactive way (maybe we will be able to translate the game into a simple application).

We hope that our initiative will not only serve to raise awareness about the issue of predatory publishing but will serve as an inspiration for all those who want to share their knowledge and create a similar teaching module.

Acknowledgements

This work was supported by project: Development of Environment for Professional Growth of the Employees of the Institute of Philosophy of the CAS' (reg. no. CZ.02.2.69/0.0/0.0/18_054/0014626).

References

Akça, S. and Akbulut, M. (2021) 'Are predatory journals contaminating science? An analysis on the Cabells' Predatory Report', *The Journal of Academic Librarianship*, 47(4), p. 102366. Available at: https://doi.org/10.1016/j.acalib.2021.102366.

Beauchamp, G. and Kennewell, S. (2010) 'Interactivity in the classroom and its impact on learning', *Computers & Education*, 54(3), pp. 759–766. Available at: https://doi.org/10.1016/j.compedu.2009.09.033.

Cahapay, M.B. (2020) 'Rethinking Education in the New Normal Post-COVID-19 Era: A Curriculum Studies Perspective', *Aquademia*, 4(2), p. ep20018. Available at: https://doi.org/10.29333/aquademia/8315.

Clapham, P. (2005) 'Publish or Perish', *BioScience*, 55(5), p. 390. Available at: https://doi.org/10.1641/0006-3568(2005)055[0390:POP]2.0.CO;2.

Elmore, S.A. and Weston, E.H. (2020) 'Predatory Journals: What They Are and How to Avoid Them', *Toxicologic Pathology*, 48(4), pp. 607–610. Available at: https://doi.org/10.1177/0192623320920209.

European Commission (2013) *Commission launches 'Opening up Education' to boost innovation and digital skills in schools and universities, European Commission - European Commission*. Available at: https://ec.europa.eu/commission/presscorner/detail/en/IP_13_859 (Accessed: 30 June 2022).

Gerashchenko, D. (2022) 'Publishing in potentially predatory journals: Do universities adopt university leaders' dishonest behavior?', *Accountability in Research*, 0(0), pp. 1–23. Available at: https://doi.org/10.1080/08989621.2022.2081916.

Interacademy Partnership (2022) *Combatting predatory academic journals and conferences: report*.

Kratochvíl, J. et al. (2020) 'Evaluation of untrustworthy journals: Transition from formal criteria to a complex view', *Learned Publishing*, 33(3), pp. 308–322. Available at: https://doi.org/10.1002/leap.1299.

Mathew, R.P., Patel, V. and Low, G. (2021) 'Predatory Journals- The Power of the Predator Versus the Integrity of the Honest', *Current Problems in Diagnostic Radiology*, p. S0363018821001389. Available at: https://doi.org/10.1067/j.cpradiol.2021.07.005.

Šímová, T., Zychová, K. and Paulová, K. (2022a) 'Stop Predatory Practice - Teaching module'. Available at: https://doi.org/10.17605/OSF.IO/GK7RH.

Šímová, T., Zychová, K. and Paulová, K. (2022b) *Stop Predatory Practices: Report from the discussion in the Czech Republic*. Zenodo. Available at: https://doi.org/10.5281/ZENODO.6038602.

Stop Predatory Practices (2022) *Stop Predatory Practices*. Available at: https://www.stoppredatorypractice.com/ (Accessed: 30 June 2022).

Think. Check. Attend. (2022) *Think Check Attend, Think Check Attend*. Available at: https://thinkcheckattend.org/ (Accessed: 5 July 2022).

Think. Check. Submit (2022) *Identify trusted publishers for your research • Think. Check. Submit., Think. Check. Submit*. Available at: https://thinkchecksubmit.org/ (Accessed: 5 July 2022).

Tsigaris, P. and Teixeira da Silva, J.A. (2021) 'Why blacklists are not reliable: A theoretical framework', *The Journal of Academic Librarianship*, 47(1), p. 102266. Available at: https://doi.org/10.1016/j.acalib.2020.102266.

UNESCO (2019) *Recommendation on Open Educational Resources (OER)*. Available at: http://portal.unesco.org/en/ev.php-URL_ID=49556&URL_DO=DO_TOPIC&URL_SECTION=201.html (Accessed: 30 June 2022).

Author Biographies

Tereza Šímová is an Open Science specialist at the Institute of Philosophy of the Czech Academy of Sciences. She is a PhD candidate at the Faculty of Economics and Management, Czech University of Life Science, where she is also a teaching librarian. In her research she focus on the use of bibliometric analysis to map the research domains. Tereza is also on the board of the Czech Association of Doctoral Researchers.

Kristýna Zychová is an Open Science Coordinator at the Czech University of Life Sciences Prague. She is also a PhD candite at the same university's Faculty of Economics and Management.

Kristýna Paulová is head of the Information Support and Education Department at the Library of the Czech University of Life Sciences in Prague. In addition, she is also the chairman of the working group for information education at the Association of University Libraries of the Czech Republic.

DEUinK: Open orchestration for capacity development nationwide

Denise Whitelock, Rebecca Ferguson, Simon Cross, Beck Pitt, Dr Fereshte Goshtasbpour, Olivier Biard
Open University, Milton Keynes, UK
denise.whitelock@open.ac.uk
rebecca.ferguson@open.ac.uk
simon.j.cross@open.ac.uk
beck.pitt@open.ac.uk
fereshte.goshtasbpour@open.ac.uk
Olivier.biard@open.ac.uk

Abstract: DEUinK is an innovative model designed to support accessible and inclusive online capacity development in eLearning for staff in Kenyan higher education institutions. The model takes research findings about how people learn online and transforms this knowledge into a practical implementation that works at scale. The approach uses 'contextualised bricolage' – drawing on the skills, resources and practices available in the Kenyan environment during implementation.

The foundations of DEUinK are:

- accessible course design and delivery, including accessible learning resources, flexible scheduling, and a distributed award system;
- technical support on an accessible learning platform that provides downloadable learning content;
- peer interaction through a community of practice that spans online and physical settings.

DEUinK has the support of the Kenyan government, which has recognised that its HE sector currently lacks sufficient expertise to design and deliver digital education, identifying this as a challenge in its National Education Sector Strategic Plan 2018-2022. The government has therefore prioritised enhancement and inclusion of eLearning as a key route to improving access to HE across Kenya. The experience of rapidly pivoting to online teaching and learning during the Covid-19 pandemic has further highlighted the need for prioritising online education. The model has high participation rates and a satisfaction rate of 98% of those recruited by Kenya Ministry of Education (n=335 and n=119 respectively)[5]. Across Kenya, 90% of eligible HEI staff have engaged with DEUinK. Participants include managers, lecturers

---

[5] Please consider the numbers in light of training-of-trainers nature of the DEUinK.

and support staff, together with experts from the Kenya Ministry of Education and Commission for University Education. For detailed evidence of impact, see impact case-study vignettes and videos. Kenyan universities are now developing training based on the DEUinK model to extend its use beyond the project. From 2023, all DEUinK resources will be openly available and supported by knowledge exchange activities, enabling educational institutions in both Kenya and other countries and from low-resourced contexts to use this model to develop staff capacity.

Introduction

Prior to the pandemic, uptake and use of online and blended forms of education were low in Kenya and most university education took place on campuses. The sudden shift to remote teaching necessitated by the pandemic highlighted the gap in staff expertise that had previously been identified in the National Education Sector Strategic Plan 2018-22. The government has therefore prioritised the enhancement and inclusion of online and distance education as a key route to improving access to HE across the country; increasing both equality and access within the sector (Kibuku *et al.*, 2020). To support the government and to enable HEI staff to move rapidly to online education while finding their voice in this new space, The Open University (UK) is leading and implementing an innovative initiative: **Digital Education for Universities in Kenya (DEUinK).** DEUinK provides an inclusive model to build expertise in accessible digital education at two levels (baseline and mastery) nationwide. The initiative which is part of the Skills for Prosperity (Kenya)[6] programme draws on global, high-quality Open Educational Resources (OER) and decades of Open University (UK) experience in online learning and teaching to close the gap in required expertise and to introduce principles of effective online education to HE staff across Kenya. The model also strengthens skills and capabilities to develop and deliver courses both at a distance and in blended contexts. DEUinK recognises that digital education requires teamwork from people in a variety of roles across the institution; it is therefore designed for educators, educational leaders and support staff, as well as those working in relevant government departments including the Ministry of Education.

Defining innovation and innovation model

DEUinK is an innovative initiative supported by the "Beyond Prototypes Model of Technology-Enhanced Learning (TEL) Innovation Process" (Scanlon *et al.*, 2013), (Figure 1). It is innovative because it has introduced to the Kenyan Higher Education community a new approach to staff development and learning that engages and

---

[6] For more information about the FCDO funded Skills for Prosperity Kenya programme (October 2020-March 2023), please see https://iet.open.ac.uk/projects/skills-for-prosperity-kenya

models digital, open online learning practices and that supports change in existing local professional practice. Methodologically, it has achieved this by creatively bringing together existing technological, pedagogical and contextual resources, frameworks and practices.

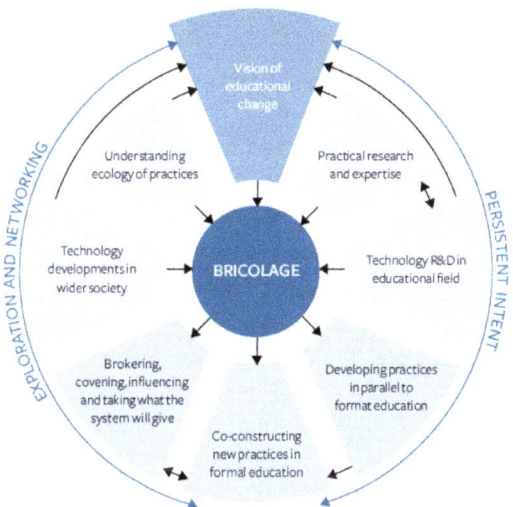

Figure 1: Beyond Prototypes Model of TEL Innovation Process (*Scanlon* et al.,2013:33)

This case history uses the Beyond Prototypes model to outline how DEUinK worked on each element in the bricolage circle to achieve a vision of educational change, build persistent intent and undertake exploration and networking.

The infrastructure

Understanding the ecology of digital education in Kenya and defining the vision of educational change- To attend to national, local and learner needs, the DEUinK vision (strengthening HE expertise in digital education) was co-created through engagement with official documents such as National Education strategic plan 2018-2022, meetings with government officials (e.g. Ministry of Education) and a needs assessment of HE staff based on the JISC Digital Capabilities Frameworks (2015; 2019a,b,c,d). In this way, gaps in expertise were identified and learning outcomes for the initiative were set.

Pedagogical research and expertise- Besides building on research and innovative pedagogies from The Open University's Institute of Educational Technology, we researched the ecology of online education in Kenyan HE using a baseline study, liaising with a Kenya-based consultant and interviewing Vice-Chancellors of public universities. This enabled us to choose the appropriate pedagogical approach while informing us of contextual challenges, such as low resources or staffing levels, to be addressed at the design stage for a successful delivery. These challenges are discussed in section 5.

Technology development in wider society (Kenya)- A major factor to consider was the use and development of technology in Kenya for educational purposes to ensure the possibility of delivering DEUinK nationwide. Constraints such as limited connectivity and access to digital devices, and weak infrastructure required design and delivery considerations which are discussed in section 5.

DEUinK bricolage and co-constructing new practices- DEUinK as a model supports accessible and inclusive online capacity development through reuse of a wide variety of OER. It draws on two key OER: a) *Take Your Teaching Online*, a badged, openly licensed course from The Open University (UK) that is hosted on the OpenLearn platform and b), JISC's (2015; 2019a,b,c,d) Digital Capabilities Framework for various HE roles, which informed the learning outcomes for DEUinK. In addition to contextualising and remixing *Take Your Teaching Online,* which included enriching and highlighting existing material on accessibility and inclusion, bespoke images were co-developed with Kenyan colleagues and incorporated into the course. Appropriate assessment and course activities were also developed to ensure relevance for all participants. A survey and evaluation supported feedback from participants.

This implemented and validated model is underpinned by "supported open learning" pedagogy (McAndrew and Weller, 2005) and is developed and delivered based on three principles to offer an accessible and inclusive suite of online training. The principles include:

Accessible and inclusive course design and delivery
Accessible approaches to teaching and learning were built into the training at design and delivery stages. These included:

Flexible schedule Participants can engage with the online training at their own pace, fitting study around work and caring commitments. This flexibility is particularly valuable for staff with disabilities such as dyslexia or long Covid that make concentrating and remembering information difficult. The options to study in short bursts and return to challenging material mean participants have the time necessary to process and engage with content.

Accessible learning resources All training content and activities meet international accessibility standards. For example, images and diagrams are accompanied by alternative text for screen readers. Videos all have transcripts. These are useful for participants with hearing issues as well as for those who do not have the bandwidth to watch a video.

Distributed award system Training includes a distributed award system of digital badges and a certificate to motivate and encourage participation and meet recognition expectations.

Inclusive technical and administrative support

To reduce anxieties related to studying online and challenges of working with a new platform, administrative and technical support was established.

Accessible learning platform The training is offered on The Open University's OpenLearn Create educational platform for open content. Core aspects of the platform are provided in ways that meet the needs of a wide variety of participants and align with international accessibility standards.

Downloadable learning content Accessing online content is difficult for those who have limited Internet access. The training is therefore available in multiple formats that can be downloaded and accessed via software, a mobile phone or an e-book reader. Participants can easily download learning resources at times when they have Internet access, and then work on them offline.

Technical team A dedicated team deal with technical and administrative issues, responding to email queries within 24 hours, and ensuring that technical issues and registration issues do not block access to training.

In-country support A Kenyan coordinator deals with inquiries and tasks that cannot be handled remotely. As well as dealing with local issues, the coordinator identified cultural and contextual factors that could limit accessibility.

Peer and community interaction

To ensure the training remains accessible and valuable, participants can join a 'community of practice' on Facebook. This community, which limits access to those involved in the initiative, has more than 280 members in public universities across the country and provides a space where participants can support each other, share ideas, resources and expertise. Specific activities in the course also encourage sharing responses in the Facebook group. Once the training comes to an end, this community will continue and be accessible to staff in all Kenyan universities.

Implementing these principles has led to a high participation rate with 90% of eligible staff participating in the training and a satisfaction rate of 98% of those recruited by Kenya's Ministry of Education. This provides other institutions with a blueprint for a highly accessible model of online capacity building for HE staff in online education.

DEUinK was developed and delivered by a team of 25 staff from four different specialist departments within The Open University (Institute of Educational Technology, The Global Development and Exchange Office, Learner and Discovery Services and the Business Innovation and Development Unit) and involves all 37 public universities in Kenya, each of which has a legal obligation to support the broader development of the country. Geographically, DEUinK covers 31 of the 47 counties in the country. The majority of the counties targeted (n=19) have a low to middle economic status.

In order to ensure this work has sustained impact across Kenya's HE sector, DEUinK has engaged governmental bodies, including the Kenya Ministry of Education and the Commission for University Education. Experts and leaders from these organisations have taken part in, publicised and helped to validate training provided by DEUinK.

The challenges

To successfully deliver DEUinK, we had to meet national and local needs, be responsive to individual participant needs, consider a range of participant levels and roles, participants' unfamiliarity with online learning, constraints on participants such as time, limited resources (broadband, devices), and the conditions caused by Covid-19. In addition, challenges related to participant motivation, retention and recognition of their achievements had to be taken into account while ensuring appropriate technical and learning support were available. Course sustainability and forward planning were further considerations.

Since DEUinK had to be offered during the demanding time of pandemic, five delivery challenges had to be taken into account: flexible scheduling, retention challenges, Internet access, participants' limited experience of online study, and consideration of inclusion & accessibility. The training had to be delivered online and offer some flexibility with minimum demand on staff workload. Thus, an asynchronous and self-paced delivery mode with reduced study hours was chosen.

There were some risks associated with retention and completion due to disruption caused by the pandemic to participants' personal and professional lives, so design principles for retention – including integrated, engaging, balanced, and reflective curriculum design – were employed. To minimise dropouts, in addition to the distributed award system, a two-week break for catching-up and processing information was built into the training. Live events were included at three critical points to provide peer and educator support.

The pandemic meant most university staff in Kenya were working off-campus. This had some connectivity and access implications (i.e., limited or unreliable internet). To address this constraint, the course was made available in multiple formats that could be downloaded and accessed via different devices.

Most participants did not have experience of online or distance learning; so an introduction to online learning was added to the training. This not only supported staff to study the course, it also prompted them to reflect on what their students would need to know in order to become effective online learners.

Learning outcomes

The DEUK initiative aimed to develop skills in relation to four areas of digital capability:

- Information, data and media literacies
- Digital creation, problem solving and innovation
- Digital learning and development
- Digital communication, collaboration and participation

The post-training survey of a sample of 119 participants reveals that participants' confidence in all these areas has increased.

Digital capability	Pre-survey (mean)	Post-survey (mean)
Produce digital material in a range of formats. • Digital creation, problem solving and innovation • Digital learning and teaching • Information, data and media literacies	3.42*	3.94
Create digital materials that meet good accessibility standards. • Digital creation, problem solving and innovation • Digital learning and teaching • Information, data and media literacies	3.31	3.99
Use accessible and inclusive forms of communication, considering the needs of different users. • Digital communication, collaboration and participation • Digital learning and teaching • Information, data and media literacies	3.42	4.03
Produce guidance and support materials related to digital services, systems and content.	3.27	3.94

Digital capability	Pre-survey (mean)	Post-survey (mean)
• Digital creation, problem solving and innovation • Digital learning and teaching • Information, data and media literacies		
Use collaborative digital environments and tools. • Digital communication, collaboration and participation • Digital learning and teaching	3.39	4.08
Use digital networks and social media to build internal or external networks. • Digital communication, collaboration and participation	3.57	4.28
Take into account students' needs and issues such as accessibility when creating digital material. • Digital creation, problem solving and innovation • Digital learning and teaching • Information, data and media literacies	3.70	4.36
Take up online professional development opportunities. • Digital learning and teaching	4.10	4.52
• Share expertise through online communities of professional learning or practice. • Digital communication, collaboration and participation	3.88	4.32
Understand and re-present information in a range of digital media • Information, data and media literacies	3.61	4.16
• Be aware of copyright laws and licensing agreements. • Information, data and media literacies (critical use)	3.71	4.32
• Evaluate digital information with an understanding of relevance, accuracy and scholarly value for the university. • Information, data and media literacies	3.76	4.31

*1=not confident at all, 5=very confident

Responses from the first set of participants (n=119) also showed that 98% of participants agreed or strongly agreed the course helped them:

- learn more about online education
- acquire knowledge and skill that is relevant to their job
- incorporate new practices related to online education/ services into their practice

The majority reported changes in perception and attitude about online learning and a shift towards learner-centred learning design. **For detailed evidence of DEUinK outcomes, see the ten impact case-study vignettes** https://bit.ly/3xgZbJR **and twelve impact videos** https://bit.ly/3wTtpSZ

How the initiative was received by participants

To date, 335 HEI staff appointed by Kenya Ministry of Education have engaged with the initiative. In addition, experts and leaders from the Kenya Ministry of Education and Commission for University Education are participating in this training for capacity development of relevant state organisations and sustainability purposes.

The post-training survey of a sample of participants (n=119) indicated that:

- 95% of participants agree or strongly agree that *the course has met their expectations.*
- 98% agree or strongly agree that DEUinK offered them an opportunity for their professional development.
- 98% agree or strongly agree that DEUinK has encouraged them to incorporate new practices related to online education/ services into my work.

Participants were also asked about the most useful features of DEUinK, which were reported as follows:

- DEUink content
- DEUink flexibility
- DEUink structure
- DEUink accessibility
- DEUink assessment
- DEUink online community of practice

What participants found most useful	Participant Feedback examples
<ul><li>Content</li><li>Use of videos and multimedia</li><li>Enriching and interactive content with practical examples</li><li>Topics covered</li><li>Clarity of content</li></ul>	*The illustrations given for each part and the practical experiences of those who have been using the online tools.* *Also the rich content and the simple language used. No IT jargons used; For me it was easy to understand most of the information.* *Introduction to the various technologies, tools and resources that I did not know they exist and empowering me to look for them and apply them in my online teaching.*
Flexibility	*The flexibility with which I could operate under was encouraging. There was no stress at all; I would repeat this over and over again.* *The flexibility in scheduling and the provision of sufficient time to read, re-read, discuss with colleagues.*

Training structure and organisation	The content is well organized and structured making it easy to read and understand.
	The way learning materials are organized in batches that are relatively easy to follow.
	The breakdown of the materials into understandable content.
Accessibility	The online platform is easily accessible with the learning materials readily available allowing one to study at their own convenient time.
	Videos with transcripts that really improved understanding of each topic
	I liked the approach that was used to develop learning material; Simple and easy to use, understand, no technical jargon, but with very helpful information some of which I used to take for granted.
Assessment	The way content summarised and the assessment included in the course.
	The quizzes at the end of each session to test my understanding.
	Quizzes were also structured in such a way that one could go back and read the notes again for greater clarity before answering the questions. The quizzes also allowed 3 attempts to answer though the marks reduced.
(Facebook) community of practice	Facebook group in exchanging new ideas.
	The Facebook community of practice and the instant response to questions in the assessment section.
	...being able to network with colleagues in online education.

Plans to further develop the initiative

DEUinK as an implemented and validated model has been successful in building capacity in eLearning at two levels of baseline and mastery in a low-resourced context. Some universities involved in the initiative, including Kibabii and Meru University, are customising the model and training to roll it out to more staff within their institutions and expand its reach. This will lead to refinements of the model and further enhance its efficiency to suit more contexts. The model has also been refined so that future projects and initiatives in Kenya and elsewhere can benefit. Based on the experience of implementing this model and different stakeholders' feedback, *Take Your Teaching Online*, the key OER on which the DEUinK model is based, has been enhanced and updated. In addition, after the project ends (March

2023), all the model and training materials will be made openly available, enabling educational institutions from other areas to reuse and remix them to develop their staff capacities.

References

JISC. (2015). *Digital Capabilities Framework*. [online] https://www.jisc.ac.uk/rd/projects/building-digital-capability.

JISC. (2019a). *Digital Leader Profile*. [online] https://repository.jisc.ac.uk/7351/1/BDCP-DL-Profile-230419.pdf

JISC. (2019b). *Learning Technology Mapping*. [online] https://repository.jisc.ac.uk/7280/1/BDCP-LTMapping-110319.pdf

JISC. (2019c). *Library and Information Professional Profile*. [online] https://repository.jisc.ac.uk/7281/2/BDCP-LIP-Profile-110319.pdf

JISC. (2019d). *Professional Services Staff in Education Profile*. [online] https://repository.jisc.ac.uk/7389/1/BDCP-PSS-Profile-300419.pdf

Kibuku, R. N., Ochieng, D. O., & Wausi, A. N. (2020). e-Learning challenges faced by universities in Kenya: A Literature Review. *Electronic Journal of e-Learning*, *18*(2), pp150-161.

McAndrew, P., Weller, M. (2005). Applying Learning Design to Supported Open Learning. In: Koper, R., Tattersall, C. (eds) Learning Design. Springer, Berlin, Heidelberg. https://doi.org/10.1007/3-540-27360-3_17

Scanlon, E., Sharples, M., Fenton-O'Creevy, M., Fleck, J., Cooban, C, Ferguson, R., Cross, S. and Waterhouse, P. (2013). *Beyond Prototypes: Enabling Innovation in Technology-enhanced Learning.* Open University, Milton Keynes. [online] http://oro.open.ac.uk/41119/1/BeyondPrototypes.pdf

National Education Sector Strategic Plan (NESSP) 2018-2022. (2018). [online] https://www.globalpartnership.org/content/kenya-national-education-sector-strategic-plan-2018-2022

Author Biographies

Professor Denise Whitelock is the Director for the Institute of Educational Technology at The Open University (UK). She is a Professor of Technology Enhanced Learning and has over twenty-five years' experience in Artificial Intelligence for designing, researching and evaluating online and computer-based learning in Higher Education.

Rebecca Ferguson is Professor of Learning Futures at The Open University in the UK. She is currently Editor in Chief of the Journal of Learning Analytics and academic lead of the FutureLearn Academic Network.

Eighth International e-Learning Excellence Awards

Simon Cross is a Senior Lecturer at the Institute of Educational Technology, the Open University, UK. He works in different geographic contexts and across a variety of digital applications exploring the intersections between assessment, digital learning, teacher professional development, open badges, learning analytics, and institutional quality enhancement.

Beck Pitt is a researcher based in the Institute of Educational Technology, The Open University (UK). A member of the award winning OER Research Hub team, Beck's current projects include Global OER Graduate Network (GO-GN) and Skills for Prosperity Kenya.

Fereshte Goshtasbpour is a lecturer in digital education at the Institute of Educational Technology (The Open University, UK). Her research focuses on learning and teaching in open and scaled online educational settings. She is particularly interested in online educators and their practices, digital technologies in higher education and technology-supported professional learning.

Olivier Biard is a Programme Manager in Global Development, Research and Knowledge Exchange at The Open University (UK). As a global development professional, he has a 22-year track record of successful partnerships that deliver change. He currently manages the implementation of strategic education programmes, in complex international and multinational contexts, including projects in the UK and Africa.

Wright School of Business Collaborative Online International Initiative: Doing Business in Peru*

Stephen Ray Smith and Amy Burger
Dalton State College, Dalton, GA, USA
ssmith@daltonstate.edu
aburger@daltonstate.edu
*We are completing work that was implemented by Dr. Carolina Duarte Hammontree. She passed away suddenly before completing the write-up of the class and data analysis. As a tribute to her and her students, we wanted her excellent work to serve as a contribution and inspiration to others.

Introduction

Almost 20 years ago, Steve Jobs famously said, "great things in business are never done by one person; they're done by a team of people" (Griggs, 2016). This statement remains true; workplaces frequently include teams of individuals with diverse cultural backgrounds. Global mindset, therefore, is important—with the rise in globalization, increasingly so. Global trade has increased significantly in the last fifty years, from 25% of international GDP in 1970 to 52% in 2020 (*The World Bank*, 2020).

According to Hofstede (1991), culture "is the collective programming of the human mind that distinguishes one group from those of another. Culture in this sense is a system of collectively held values" (p. 4). Understanding other cultures provides background information as well as sensitivity towards individuals and organizations that foster collaborative decision-making and strengthens group efficacy. Because the United States covers such a vast land area and primarily uses a single language, most citizens, and especially students, have a less well-developed understanding and appreciation of other cultures. Conversely, Europeans, for example, often acquire multiple languages, travel significantly, interact with various ethnic and religious groups, and experience the vagaries of culture from very early ages as a basic part of simply living in the environment. American students often are unaware of the significance of globalization (Lane and Murphrey, 2020). So, providing additional opportunities for American students to develop a global mindset enables them to participate more fully in the global arena.

Higher education enables students to develop competencies sought by employers (MacDermott and Ortiz, 2017). Therefore, graduating students moving into the labor force benefit from coursework that prepares them for the demands of their future workplace (Nealy, 2020). Because of the importance of global mindset in today's workplaces, international educational experiences are increasingly valuable to students.

Internationalization has been a long-term goal of almost every business school. It is frequently one of the major program goals for AACSB-accredited institutions. In fact, the 2020 AACSB Accreditation standards note that business schools, through their impact, "should make a difference in business and society as well as in the global community of business schools" (AACSB, 2022, p. 10). One of the ways to impact and internationalize students has frequently been through study abroad experiences, either for a short-term experience, or a longer-term, often semester-long exchange, with various partner institutions across the globe.

Curricular international experience can take many forms: lectures, writing, excursions, readings, activities, research, group projects, service learning, and more (Lane and Murphrey, 2020). Such activities show promise for the development of a global mindset by providing students with opportunities for international engagement through meaningful, content-driven interaction with peers from other countries (Larson and Baburaj, 21).

While students may not understand the value of international experience to their future goals (Curtis and Ledgerwood, 2018), Lane and Murphrey (2020) suggest that the benefits of international experiences can be grouped into categories: personal growth, international knowledge, cultural awareness, and additional skills. These qualities benefit stakeholders, including institutions, students, and their eventual employers.

Study abroad is a common way students gain international experience. Students who participate benefit from improved academic achievement, increased rates of retention and graduation, and improved outcomes in the job market (Oberhelman and Dunn, 2019); Larson and Baburaj (2020) note that college graduates "with skills learned from international experiences" are in high demand in the job market (p. 16). But international experiences have value that goes beyond workplace competency; additional benefits include enhanced learning, critical thinking, relationship-building, leadership skills, and improved cultural familiarity (Larson and Baburaj, 2020). Study abroad is also a high impact practice, which research shows "increase rates of student retention and student engagement" (Kuh, 2008, p. 9).

For many students, however, international travel is out of reach. Research by Lane and Murphrey (2020) identified several barriers to student participation, including cost and conflicts with work, extracurricular, or academic obligations. While short-term study abroad has been used as a more affordable alternative to semester- or year-long exchanges (Hallows *et al.*, 2011), limitations to travel resulting from circumstances such as global crises have historically been an additional barrier to international study (Mercado, 2020). The recent COVID-19 pandemic, with widespread effects, sparked an increase in the acceptability of alternatives to international travel and study abroad (Mescon, 2020). Additionally, at schools like Dalton State College (DSC) in Dalton, GA, the state's only Hispanic Serving Institution (HSI) with a large population of first-generation and lower income students, bringing collaborative online international experiences to campus is more feasible and scalable, so, like some other similar colleges, DSC has turned to alternative classroom-based initiatives to encourage students to develop intercultural understanding.

The primary focus of this study was to encourage the development of global mindset among undergraduate business students. Research findings could offer valuable insights into how business schools can internationalize some existing courses by using collaborative online international programs to help students develop their global mindset. The Wright School of Business (WSOB) at DSC is part of the University System of Georgia (USG) in the United States. The WSOB is committed to implementing innovative instructional practices to enhance students' awareness of the global environment of business. To improve students' global mindset, WSOB entered into partnerships with several business schools across Latin America, including Peru, Venezuela, Dominican Republic, Mexico, Argentina and Chile. Because the pandemic significantly altered plans for international travel to partner institutions, WSOB utilized existing technology to maintain program viability through virtual practices to enable collaborative course offerings at no additional costs to either students or participating institutions.

One program between Peru's Pontificia Universidad Catolica del Peru and DSC entitled "Doing Business in Peru" provided students with an opportunity to explore entrepreneurial landscapes in the emerging Peruvian marketplace. The program's primary goal was to offer students an international and multicultural experience to improve and expand their global mindset.

The virtual program incorporated online platforms and innovative methodologies to increase WSOB's internationalization efforts. This program was developed under the guidance of the dean of the business school, the office of international education, and the international education committee. The project was aligned with the WSOB's strategic plan regarding international education. The program's mission was to create opportunities to promote the participation of our faculty and students in online international educational programs between the WSOB and foreign universities. The program was designed to enhance, throughout collaboration in international real-life business projects and virtual experiences, faculty and students' global learning experience, research opportunities, and international network. Moreover, because the program was created in a fully online and multicultural environment, the students have the opportunity to develop new professional skills analyzing complex issues in other nations.

For students, the program was designed to offer an international and multicultural dimension within a virtual format in order to expand their global mindset. To achieve this, we created a simulated business working environment in which DSC students represented an American company considering expanding operations to Peru. The Peruvian students represented a consulting firm to provide potential investors with information about the country and the feasibility of doing business there.

The infrastructure

The people involved in the activity were lead faculty members from PUCP and DSC. Each was teaching an international business course in the same semester, roughly scheduled for the same time of day and days of the week. Prior to the in-class live activity, a librarian visited the class to provide support for preliminary research on international business using resources including the CIA World Factbook, the World Trade Organization, the United Nations, and the World Bank.

The activity was facilitated with the use of Zoom web conferencing software, which students accessed via their own devices.

The challenges

One practical challenge was the difference in time zone. DSC students were told to join the link at 9 am, but for PUCP students this was 8 am. Being clear about the time of the activity was essential to avoid confusion. Additionally, the class schedules of the institutions were not aligned exactly, meaning one group of students would join early in their normal class meeting time, while the other group may have had some class activity prior to the start of the activity.

An unexpected and tragic challenge arose with the sudden death of DSC's lead faculty member for the activity, which occurred later in the semester after the synchronous virtual activity. This resulted in another faculty member taking on the class and subsequent planning for the semester as well as for future semesters. We continue our colleague's work in an effort to honor her legacy to her students as well as her passion for international business and preparing the next generation to embrace a global mindset. Dalton State College is a Hispanic Serving Institution (HSI) as about 36% of our student population is Hispanic and first generation university students. Rather than accept the setback from the pandemic that effectively shut down international travel to our partner institutions, we explored alternative ways and means to accomplish our objectives, and this program which is continuing offered the best, non-additional cost alternative. The results were sufficiently positive that we are strengthening our partnerships and adding other functions to the program.

How the initiative was received by the users or participants

The Spring 2021 collaboration provided an excellent international learning experience that positively impacted over 80 students. A simple yet significant outcome of the first session was that students used social media accounts such as Instagram and LinkedIn to communicate throughout the remainder of the program. This activity had a positive reception; students connected with each other and created a Whatsapp group to communicate after the project was over. Additionally, the responses to the survey distributed to participants was a rich source of information about the student experience.

The learning outcomes

Concluding the program, professors crafted and administered a survey to both Peruvian and American students to measure the impact of the learning experience. The program was evaluated primarily through two research tools: the application of a pre and post-global mindset survey and the administration of a survey to measure students and faculty' satisfaction with the program. After organizing the data and reviewing the transcribed database and coding, the following themes emerged: **Empathy in understanding other perspectives**

> "It helped a good bit. I have never worked with students outside of the US before, and this changed my perspective."

> "To grow culturally."

> "It helped me realize that not every country around the world has the same tools and opportunities that we do in the US."

Knowledge of global issues

"It helped me gain a better understanding of life in a foreign [sic] country. With the election going on in Peru, we had a great opportunity to learn about how officials can affect businesses in a foreign [sic] country."

"Having someone that is in the country and experiences everything that is going on firsthand is very insightful, I made friends, and I learned more of the political, economic, and social aspect of Peru."

Connection with international peers

"The Peruvian students were very helpful, and we even talked way past the class time."

"Being able to speak to foreign [sic] students my age was very helpful."

Belief in this activity's application for workplace skills

"It was preparatory for the work I will do after graduation."

"I liked how in the near future I could possibly do business internationally."

"Helped me learn about a whole different country and the possibilities of possibly doing business in the future"

Additionally, many DSC students expressed interest in learning Spanish as a second language.

Plans to further develop the initiative

One program planned subsequent to the activity later in the same semester was an event called "Meet and Talk," an informal virtual conversation for students to practice their foreign language skills while socializing with international peers.

We hope to continue the activity with PUCP and/or other institutions. We may also try reversing the roles in the simulation for a project in which a foreign company considers investing in the U.S., putting DSC students in the role of consultants.

International experiences are valuable to college students' development of a global mindset, which is increasingly important to the job market into which they will graduate and begin their careers. While international travel has long been considered the primary way for students to gain cultural knowledge, it has limitations and costs that make it inaccessible to many, the pandemic and subsequent travel restrictions increased barriers to student access. The Internet, however, provides an opportunity for increased innovation in this area. Through a collaboration between international partner institutions and the use of a COIL activity, undergraduate business students from two countries participated in a virtual exchange designed to encourage the development of global mindset. Qualitative data analysis suggests that the activity was effective and found to be valuable by student participants.

Business schools are educating the future business leaders of our global community. Students are expected to enhance their international leadership skills and understand the main challenges of global business. We live in a global business world. There is a high probability that our business students will be doing business with suppliers and customers from other countries. Therefore, partnerships and collaborative programs with international universities will help business students enhance their international business and multicultural skills, preparing them to make informed and sustainable business decisions. Thus, we are strengthening the decision-making process of our business students to help them become productive global citizens.

The Collaborative Online International Learning Program (COIL) is applicable and affordable for any business school. The focus of this international strategy requires building a global network with faculty members from universities across the globe and from countries that are relevant to each institution's strategic goals. For example, DSC has engaged in developing partnerships with AACSB business schools in Latin American which are opening further opportunities for online international collaborations to improve students' global mindset, to further internationalize course offerings at DSC, and to increase faculty and students' international network.

References

AACSB. (2022), "2020 guiding principles and standards for business accreditation", available at: https://www.aacsb.edu/-/media/documents/accreditation/2020-aacsb-business-accreditation-standards-jul-1-2022.pdf?rev=4664d28a4366497cb804183fe24dd1e4&hash=9860B587B7327C9AF58C6D7ACD1AA54E (accessed 18 July 2022)

Curtis, T. and Ledgerwood, J. R. (2018), "Students' motivations, perceived benefits and constraints towards study abroad and other international education opportunities", *Journal of International Education in Business*, Vol. 11 No. 1, pp. 63-78.

Griggs, B. (2016), "10 great quotes from Steve Jobs", available at: https://www.cnn.com/2012/10/04/tech/innovation/steve-jobs-quotes/index.html (accessed 18 July 2022).

Hallows, K., Paige, P. W., and Marks, M. A. (2011), "Short-term study abroad: a transformational approach to global business education", *Journal of International*

Education in Business, Vol. 4 No. 2, pp. 88-111. https://doi.org/10.1108/18363261111189504

Hofstede, G. (1991), *Cultures and organizations: software of the mind*. McGraw-Hill, London.

Kuh, G. (2008), *High-impact educational practices: what they are, who has access to them, and why they matter*. Association of American Colleges and Universities, Washington, DC.

Lane, K. and Murphrey, T. P. (2020), "Benefits of and best practices for international experiences for college students: a synthesis of the literature", *Journal of International Agricultural and Extension Education*, Vol. 27 No. 4, pp. 39-61.

Larson, B. V. and Baburaj, Y. (2020), "Alternative multi-mode international learning: a model establishing collaboration", *Journal of International Business Disciplines*, Vol. 15 No. 1, pp. 15-28.

MacDermott, C. and Ortiz, L. (2017), "Beyond the business communication course: a historical perspective of the where, why, and how of soft skills development and job readiness for business graduates", *IUP Journal of Soft Skills* Vol. 11 No. 2, pp. 7-24.

Mercado, S. (2020), "International student mobility and the impact of the pandemic", available at: https://www.aacsb.edu/insights/articles/2020/06/covid-19-and-the-future-of-international-student-mobility (accessed 19 July 2022)

Mescon, T. (2020), "Global connection in times of reduced mobility", available at: https://www.aacsb.edu/insights/articles/2020/06/global-connection-in-times-of-reduced-mobility (accessed 19 July 2022)

Nealy, C. (2020), "Authentic engagement through workplace pedagogy", *Administrative Issues Journal,* Vol. 10 No. 2, pp. 19-32.

Oberhelman, S. M. and Dunn, C. A. (2019), "Globally networked learning in a university classroom: a pilot program", *Athens Journal of Education,* Vol. 6 No. 1, pp. 1-12.

The World Bank. (2022), "Trade (% of GDP)", available at: https://data.worldbank.org/indicator/NE.TRD.GNFS.ZS (accessed 19 July 2022)